The EXIT Formula

How To Sell Your Business For 3x More Than It's Worth Today

By
Mike Warren

Copyright © 2015 Mike Warren

Published by *Accelerated Publishing Inc.*

ISBN-13:978-1508836018
ISBN-10:1508836019

Legal Disclaimer

All Rights Reserved. No part of this publication may be reproduced in any form or by any means, including scanning, photocopying, or otherwise without prior written permission of the copyright holder.

Disclaimer and Terms of Use: The Author and Publisher have strived to be as accurate and complete as possible in the creation of this book, notwithstanding the fact that they do not warrant or represent at any time that the contents within are accurate due to the rapidly changing nature of the Internet. While all attempts have been made to verify the information provided in this publication, the Author and Publisher assume no responsibility for errors, omissions, or contrary interpretation of the subject matter herein. Any perceived slights of specific persons, peoples, or organizations are unintentional. In practical advice books, like anything else in life, there are no guarantees of income made. Readers are cautioned to rely on their own judgment about their individual circumstances to act accordingly. This book is not intended for use as a source of legal, business, accounting or financial advice. All readers are advised to seek services of competent professionals in the legal, business, accounting, and finance fields.

The EXIT Formula

Table of Contents

Introduction v

Chapter 1: The Realities of Today's Marketplace 1

Chapter 2: The Business Owner's Preferred Outcome 5

Chapter 3: Why You Need A Business Growth Hacking Expert On Your Team First 15

Chapter 4: Creating Your Sales Team 21

Chapter 5: Methods of Selling Your Business 25

Chapter 6: The Realistic Value of Your Business Today 29

Chapter 7: Methods to Increase the Value of Your Business 33

Chapter 8: Lack of Marketing Can Kill Your business Growth 39

Chapter 9: Talented People Work for Growing Companies 47

Chapter 10: Systemizing Your Business 53

Chapter 11: Capital Comes In Many Different Forms 69

Chapter 12: Getting More Customers 73

Chapter 13: Finishing the Process Increases Your Bottom Line 83

Chapter 14: Customer Retention 93

Chapter 15: Networking Your Way to Millions 99

Chapter 16: How To Get All the Guidance You Need 109

Conclusion 113

Bonus Chapter 115

About The Author 121

The EXIT Formula

The EXIT Formula

Introduction

Thank you for making the decision to take a few minutes out of your busy day to learn a few secrets that until now I have been reluctant to share with the general public. I decided to finally write this book to give you a behind the scenes look at some of the ways that we take companies to the next level. I will be "opening the kimono" (so to speak) and sharing secrets that will help you to grow your company.

I have a couple of goals that I hope to attain with this book. First, I will be showing you how to increase the profits of any company, regardless of the industry, and how to do it in a relatively short period of time. The timeframe I am talking about is only a short 12-18 months. Part of my business is to buy and sell companies. I have teams that take what I am about to share with you and implement these techniques to obtain "hyper" growth in a company (maybe even your own).

Secondly, companies that I buy or partner with want me to implement these strategies on their behalf since we have the skills, manpower, and resources to make it happen without dramatically changing how the business operates. I want to show how you, too, can become one of the lucky few who benefit.

I get excited every time I think about the number of people we help who have transformed their companies into the powerhouse they knew it could be and received the financial rewards they have been waiting for.

I am talking about "Hyper Growth." Some people in our industry have even referred to it as "Growth Hacking." Every company we have purchased or partnered with have all had some of the same

The EXIT Formula

fundamental issues. It doesn't matter if your company is doing $100,000 a year in sales or $30 million. These strategies are needed to take any company to the next level.

We all know that The American Dream has always been to own a house. I'm not saying that the Dream is gone, but topping the dream of homeownership today is the dream of getting rid of the job and being your own boss.

That dream includes having a business that provides you with a six or seven figure income each year to support the lifestyle that you want, doing the things you want to do with the people you want to do those things with, and no longer having money be the big issue.

If you have ever dreamed of growing your business and then selling it for a lot more than it is worth today, then you have found the book you have been looking for. This book covers the basics of how to obtain hyper growth of companies that you currently own, work for or want to buy and resell.

I'll be answering some of the most common questions that people ask me in my seminars or from some of my high-level coaching students. I will be sharing my expert techniques to help you analyze the best methods to use for your business to obtain hyper-growth.

The whole "hunt" leading up to the sale is, for me, as exciting as the "kill" (the sale). Because of this, I am always looking at every business I encounter as a potential business to growth hack. Whether these are ones that are brought to me for help or ones that I come across in everyday life, I am always looking at how they operate, what their strengths are, what they could be doing better and what I would do if I were them.

The EXIT Formula

Businesses themselves always get me thinking. It's how I get my buzz!

So please sit back and keep reading. Your future success lies in these pages.

Mike Warren

The EXIT Formula

Chapter 1

The Realities of Today's Marketplace

One of the most disheartening industry statistics that I have seen is that as few as 15% of all businesses are ever sold.

The other 85% simply fade away, are closed by the owners because they couldn't sell, or go out of business and have their assets liquidated.

Too often, owners want to sell, but can't get the price that they need. They hang on, hoping for a better price, long after running the business has stopped being fun. They rarely get the price and the business survives until the owners get tired and close it.

The information you're about to learn in this book will show you how to not only ensure that you're in that lucky 15% that are able to sell their businesses, but also how to prepare your business so that it sells for the maximum amount possible and under the best circumstances for you.

I am willing to bet that if a poll were taken with business owners, the statistics would indicate an overwhelming majority who would be willing, under the right conditions, to sell their business immediately. There are many reasons for this, such as:

- Owners that are tired of doing the same thing
- Pending or planned retirement
- Cashing out
- Hours too tiring
- A desire to try something different
- They haven't obtained what they thought the business would

deliver (this is not an indication of a bad business... just maybe a bad owner).

While there are no such polls, you can imagine that, under the right conditions, every owner would sell. Wouldn't you? Having acknowledged this, it is important for you to keep this in mind as you prepare your business to sell. I have seen too many businesses that seem to have all of the ingredients for success but are only marginally successful and businesses that that seem to be successful (or at least are still in business) despite themselves.

You can improve any business. You will become tuned into this, and it's actually quite fun. Taking a business and growing it through planning, networking and the implementation of ideas is the most fascinating thing that I can think of doing.

Why Do You Want To Sell Your Business?

This is the first question that every buyer wants to have answered, but even more importantly, it's the question that you need to answer for yourself.

The answer to this question will tell you when you should sell, how you should sell, and most importantly, if it is even possible to sell your business at all.

Business owners have many varied reasons for selling their companies. A business sale may be the logical conclusion of a long and successful business.

For some, the sale may be motivated by circumstances outside of their control like a personal or family crisis. For others, it may be brought on

The EXIT Formula

by a change in business conditions. Then there are those that just want a total change or new opportunity.

The reason for selling is often a critical part of in the sales process. Business sales are typically strategic transactions, and the outcome will inevitably be influenced by your sale motivations.

To exit your business successfully the very first step you must accomplish is to identify the specific reasons that have brought you to the decision to sell your company. You must find the *true reason* why you're interested in selling your company. If you don't find your *true reason* then this may cost you severely, or possibly even keep you from selling your business altogether. An honest answer is important for your prospective buyers, but it's even more critical for you to determine how best to move ahead in the selling process.

The EXIT Formula

Chapter 2

The Business Owner's Preferred Outcome

The new American Dream would be to have an unsolicited offer of purchase for over the true market value of the business, with all-cash and an immediate closing. We would all like to live to be 150 years old, but I sincerely doubt that either one is ever going to happen!

All prudent sellers want to receive the best price possible when they sell their business, but from experience I can tell you that this is only one of the priorities that sellers want to receive when they sell.

They are also concerned with the timing of the sale, what will happen in the future to the business they've poured so much time and effort into, and how their future will be impacted by the terms of the sale.

Too often tax considerations are not considered until the deal has been structured. Careful structuring of the deal can often reduce the tax bite at sale.

There is an old adage: "A seller can eat well or he can sleep well, but he can't do both." That refers to the choice that sellers often face - get a great price with huge risk, or a lower price safely.

While that adage is often true, it is important to recognize that the seller can often get the best of both worlds. That is one of the things that my book shows you how to do.

It's imperative that you fully understand your reasons for selling in order to determine which factors are critically important to you and which ones you can be more flexible on.

Many business owners feel that they need to sell fast. The reason that this may be critical to them could be caused by sickness or death, being burned out and not having the energy they think is necessary for the business to continue to grow and be successful in the coming years. Other circumstances could include the transfer of a spouse to a new location, cash to solve other nonbusiness related problems or a myriad of other nonbusiness reasons. This type of seller will probably take the first buyer who comes along and offers modest, but acceptable price, even though they could hold out and sell for much more.

Then there is the seller who is willing to take a long-term view and isn't pressured to make a fast sale. Since they don't have an urgent need to sell, they can afford to take the time necessary to maximize the benefits from the sale of their business. They are willing to stay involved with the company for as long as it takes for them to get the results they're looking for. They have very different motives for selling. Their motivation may be just to take some money off the table for future retirement or to diversify the hard work that they put into their business with other investments to secure their financial future.

This type of seller is usually interested in more than just the money. They would like to see the company they created have a strong and successful future. They often want loyal employees to benefit as well. Typically, they're willing to stay on for a period of time after the sale to help the purchaser successfully take control of the company. They also tend to be more receptive to owner financing since they will be there to help ensure the safety of their investment. (In a worst case scenario, where the owner has to take back his company, he has gotten the benefits of the improvements/innovations made, and is usually much better off than before he started the sales process.)

This difference in motivation typically results in the quick sale all-cash seller receiving much less for the sale of their company than the strategically oriented seller.

The EXIT Formula

One of the important things to take away from the above is that your motivations and their implications can have a large effect on the ultimate benefit you get from selling.

Putting Your Priorities in Perspective

The following will help to define the variables that will shape your sale strategy:
- Asking price relative to the marketplace
- Seller financing or all-cash
- Staying involved (or not) after closing
- Timing of the sale
- Involvement after the sale (immediate departure vs. ongoing involvement)
- How customers and employees may react to the sale

There will also be conflicts which are based in part on which of your motivations are the most important to you. As I said before, it would be nice to achieve an immediate, all-cash sale at a high selling price, but it's unlikely that you will get that type of offer. I can't stress enough how conflicting priorities can possibly derail the ultimate sale of your company.

Here are some of the more common problems a misalignment of priorities can cause:

1. **Fast Sale, High Price, and All-Cash.** Hoping for this type of offer is only going to lead you to disappointment. Any intelligent buyer that's aware of the realities in the marketplace is just not going to make an offer like this, so throw this out to the wayside. There is a myth that a private equity group with hugh cash reserves will buy your company at top dollar. This very rarely happens. Private equity groups are smart people who

make their living by buying bargains. Paying a buyer to pdollar is not part of their business model.
2. **High Price *and* an Immediate Departure**. A seller that wants just to take the money and run raises all kinds of red flags for the buyer. They get the feeling that the seller is hiding something that will be detrimental to the business. Buyers like when a seller has "skin in the game." Buyers will usually pay a premium for that "skin." Conversely, they will demand a discount for a buyer who wants a quick exit.
3. **Immediate Departure and Minimal Disruption to the Business**. Requesting conditions like these that are in direct conflict with each other are very limiting on the buyers future potential for the business and will kill your sale fast.

One of the most effective strategies for eliminating most, if not all, conflicts is to work with a business growth hacking expert to prepare your business for its future sale. If you allow enough time to plan and prepare for the sale, you can address and fix any possible motivational conflicts you might have to ensure that you are able to sell your business for the most benefit possible to you. Nobody knows your business as well as you do. Buyers know that. The more willing that you are to stay for some period of time to assist in the transition, the happier the buyer is. That happiness (and the security that the seller's presence provides) often translates to a higher sales price.

Obviously you don't want to lie, but there is a right and a wrong way for you to answer. Answers like "I want to slow down a bit" or "I want to travel" or "we've got a baby on the way and I want to spend more time at home" communicate to a potential buyer that you plan on winding down when they take over. What they want to hear is your intention to help them realize the potential locked inside your business. Here are some suggested responses based on your age:

- **If you are under 40,** you clearly aren't ready to "retire" so you need to communicate that you see an upside in merging your business with theirs:
  "In order for us to get to the next level we need to find a partner with more (sales people, distribution, geographic reach, capital or whatever the partner brings to the table)" -whatever the appropriate answer is for your circumstances
- **If you are between 40-55** years old, most people will understand the need to shore up your personal balance sheet:
  "I've reached a time in my life where I want to create some liquidity from the value I've created so far, and at the same time I want to find a partner who can help us get to the next level."
- **If you are over 55,** you can start to talk about retirement, but you want to make sure you communicate that you still have lots of energy and passion for your business:
  "I'm at a stage where I need to start thinking about retirement. It's a long way off yet, but I want to be proactive."

Finding the Right Answers

There are so many reasons why someone sells a business: retirement, illness, boredom, new opportunities, chance to cash out, divorce, relocation, etc. Whatever the reason, there has been a conscious decision made that they no longer want it. The driving force behind the decision is the realization that the rewards they are reaping are not commensurate with their efforts. If they were, chances are they would not be selling.

I am always leery of any reason that someone gives for selling his or her business, except for the desire to "cash out" or my personal preference - the morbid reasons: death, divorce, illness. Think about

The EXIT Formula

it: if the business was rewarding the Seller for what they felt was the effort that he/she was expending, wouldn't they want to keep it going for themselves or their family? That is why the reason of "other business interests" usually causes me to question their motives further. Notwithstanding this, there is much leverage to be gained by their decision. Selling a business for most people is a difficult decision and one that will have taken a lot of time to make.

Once the decision has been made, it is, in most cases, something the Seller wants to complete.

If the owner says that their reasoning is new opportunities, boredom, or the business needs "new blood," this will alarm the buyer... These reasons simply do not portray the viability of the business. It is a warning flag for buyers to dig, dig, and dig for details.

Whatever your answer is, you must be prepared to answer these questions a buyer may ask:

Reason: Retirement, Illness Questions
- What are you planning to do?
- Will you be staying in this area?
- Are you looking forward to it?
- Do you think you'll miss the business?
- Has it prevented you from devoting full time to the business?
- For how long?
- Is there a chance that you may want to rejoin the business later?
- Does this situation mean any specific timing issues that I should be aware of?
- What is it that the business does not provide for you?
- Is it simply a matter that you have been doing this too long?
- If the business is so good, why not get someone to run it and

split the profits?
- Is it a similar business? (Other Business Interests)
- Can't you do both?
- Do you have to sell this one to begin the other?
- Does that mean that this business cannot grow to your expectations?

Reason: Boredom, New Opportunity, Cash out, Divorce/Partner, Relocation
- Are you planning to start another venture?
- How flexible are you on the terms?
- Why don't you buy them out?
- Do they have shares in the company?
- What percentage?
- Must they approve any deal we make?
- Why can't you move the business?
- What are you going to do in your new city?

On the flip side, here are some of my favorite "buying "questions:
- *What "keeps you up at night" about the business?*
  Every business owner has concerns, regardless of how successful he/she may be. This question will, in most cases, serve to identify what the current owner deems to be the biggest threat to the company. If they tell you "nothing," or their "spouse's snoring," you want to reword the question to be: "If you were not selling the business, what would be your biggest concerns about the daily operations and future for this company?"
- *How much vacation do you take?*
  You are not asking this because you want time off even though you haven't started yet. In fact, it's the opposite. If they tell you none to less than two weeks a year, then you know that

the business is clearly not employee-driven. This can be due to many reasons: lack of trust, poor employees, and the owner is – or thinks they are – "the business," workaholic syndrome, or the Seller just does not believe that the business can survive, let alone thrive, without his or her presence.

This would be a good time to ask: "What would happen to the business if you got hit by a truck tomorrow?" or "I was hoping that this business would, in time, allow me to take 4- 6 weeks of vacation. Is this possible?" Again, you are probing. You will be surprised to hear many owners tell you (without even realizing it) that, in their mind, the employees are simply not capable of running the business without the Seller being present. This is another "flag." Right or wrong, it will tell you whether the employees will welcome someone who will encourage an environment of growth and recognition of their efforts.

In this case, they will "run through fire" for you. Alternatively, maybe the owner is right, and they are not capable. This will mean changes are needed. Only you can decide this.

- *What would your customers and competitors say the business does best?*

The answer you get from the owner is most likely what he believes the customers and/or competitors will say. In addition, the Seller will say what he believes are the strengths of the business. When you embark on the investigation and Due Diligence period, pay particular attention to the Seller's answer versus reality. It will give you a very good indication if the company has been successful implementing and executing its Marketing and Business Plans.

- *Why do your customers buy from you?*

See if the Seller can reduce this to one answer or at least rank them. Remember, someone is trying to sell you something so they will probably give you all kinds of reasons. In most cases, the Seller's answers do not mirror what the customers would really say.

- *What are the biggest challenges facing the business for the future?*
  As mentioned previously, Sellers will generally be honest but guarded when it comes to criticizing and analyzing their own business. This is common in many businesses. They do not perform regular evaluations to see where they are, what they've done, what's working, what's not, or they do not conduct realistic self-evaluations. Do not fall into the same trap once you own the business. Ongoing evaluation is critical.

  When you pose this question, be sure to take good notes (as usual). You may be lucky enough to gain some tremendous insight. Every business faces challenges, and who better to pinpoint them than the owner (if they can do so objectively)? If you get an answer, that does not outline what these challenges are, be wary. Interestingly enough, the owner's opinion on this may differ dramatically from what you will learn from the employees or on your own. If you are not satisfied with the response that the Seller provides, press them for a more elaborate explanation. Surely there must be challenges! Get specific. Ask questions related to sales, marketing, product development, marketplace, etc.

- **My favorite**: *Are they open to a possible partnership?*
  Chances are they will flatly refuse this. Why would they want a partner when they are trying to sell the whole business? They will probably say that they have run the business alone, and they cannot see themselves in a partnership situation. Realize

The EXIT Formula

that, as a minority partner, I am not buying a job. I am bringing my resources, networks and ability to grow the business to the table, and I will be paid accordingly.

Chapter 3

Why You Need A Business Growth Hacking Expert On Your Team First

At the same time that I was doing real estate, I was also a Systems Engineer. So I was working full time, I was in real estate full time, and I was going to school full time. I was a little bit of an overachiever. I was not married, had no kids at the time, so I guess I could afford to do a little bit of that. I just wanted all the different things at one time, so I got an Associate's degree in Computer Science. I also got a Bachelor's degree in Management Information Systems. Along the way, I found out that I was an okay engineer, but I wasn't a great engineer. I started to find out that I actually had a lot more passion and that I was much better at real estate and business than I was as an engineer. The company I worked for wanted me to really focus on engineering, but I was starting to slowly shift my focus from engineering to the business side of things.

Ultimately I had to make a decision on my own that I wanted to do real estate and business. When I started years ago in the foreclosure arena, I was looking at different courses and materials that I could buy. I was spending money buying anything and everything, trying to get my knowledge going. With all this valuable information that I accumulated I always had mentors along the way, whether I was working in real estate, general business or internet marketing. I have always tried to seek out the experts. To have access to the top people sometimes requires a cash outlay, which in the end is well worth it. I learned early on that I had to spend a little bit of money to gain more knowledge. (Full disclosure…I probably spend about $300,000 a year on coaching and mentoring.)

The EXIT Formula

Over the next ten years or so I was watching what my mentors were doing. I was getting very successful in real estate. I was doing a lot of things. I started looking at buying real estate. Then I graduated to buying and profiting from the paper that's attached to property. Buying a piece of real estate, rehabbing it, and then reselling it is a lot of work. But I found that I could actually purchase a paper, or a mortgage, or a lien on a property, and make sometimes as much money than I would if I had bought it and rehabbed and resold it. But I wouldn't have all those headaches. So I started looking at buying paper and going that route.

Along that same time we had the savings and loan crisis, which led to the creation of the Resolution Trust Corporation. The Resolution Trust Corporation was a government entity that essentially took over all of the assets of all of these collapsed savings and loans, so it included mortgages, it included houses, it included raw land, and it included commercial buildings. So the Resolution Trust Corporation was mandated to go out and sell all those things. I actually started learning how to buy from the Resolution Trust Corporation. I began in a down market when property values were continuously plummeting and the economy was hurting and over time as the market improved, I found that this was even easier in a better market. But I still did well.

Management Is Where It's At

After I had finished my undergraduate degree, I started looking into Management Information Systems. As I began looking at more of the managing side, I felt that there was a stronger pull for me to go into that realm. I also started looking at and reading the Wall Street Journal, Forbes, and similar publications and realized that the money was being made in business. There's a lot of money in real estate, but really the big bucks, these $20, $30, $50 billion deals are being done with business - buying and selling companies.

I decided to go back to school to learn how to buy and sell companies, but nobody actually taught that. I knew I had to go and get a finance degree and try to learn a little bit of it. I figured I would go to school, get a finance degree, go work for Merrell Lynch or Lehman Brothers or Goldman Sachs, or any of these bigger type investment firms that also did all of these IPOs and buying and selling of these companies. It quickly dawned on me when I was in school that trying to go into one of those companies would not afford me the opportunity to be able to start anywhere near the top. I'd essentially be starting in the mail room, even though I'd have my MBA. If you don't have a degree from Harvard or Yale or Wharton, one of the top three or four schools, odds are that you weren't going to get in at any kind of real level. I was going to have to work my way up, and my personality wouldn't let me wait that long.

I started to think about who I knew, or who could find someone that knows some of this stuff. That led me to another mentor who was also doing real estate, but he was also doing this whole other business of buying companies. He actually owned 20 or 30 different companies. I was always curious as to how a person could do that. How can you manage those things? How can you make these things grow?

So here I was, still finishing graduate school and working in finance and real estate. I figured I would always be doing real estate because I was making enough money in it, so why would I ever stop? However, I started looking at how I could start buying and selling companies.

When I was talking with my mentor, he showed me a little bit about the business side. I found out that you can buy and grow companies,

The EXIT Formula

although it can take years and years, but the payoffs can be really good. The key ingredient is buying a company and not running it yourself. It's really about the people; finding the right people who can go into the company for you and run it for you, so that you can, kind of like *Rich Dad* says, hit that fourth quadrant. You become a business owner, an investor, where your money that you invest in these companies grows for you and somebody else does the work. You are essentially creating passive income.

It is the same thing when you do real estate. It is passive income. If you buy a property and you rent it out, that rental income that comes in is passive income, which is nice because it is taxed differently as well (the deductions). It's easy money. I was chatting with my mentor and figuring out how I could apply that to what I was doing within the real estate world. What I figured out in real estate was that I could buy houses with no money down. It was about how creative I could get on any deal whether it was a residential deal or a commercial deal. It didn't matter the size. It's just a matter of me figuring out what was the need of the owner of those properties, and then I could create an offer that would match that need. So long as I could still make money with it, it was worthwhile. It became a win-win situation.

Over a period of time working with my mentor, one of the things I figured out is that I could take the same ideas that he's doing with his businesses, and I could combine what I was already doing with real estate, which is the whole creative no money downside, and I could combine the two of them together. I started tweaking and testing different things to see if this was possible to do. Can you buy a company with no money down? How do you do that? Like in real estate, I could purchase a house with no money down, meaning that I could take over an existing debt that's on the house, such as the mortgage, and if there's any money left over I could get the owner to carry a note for the difference for another mortgage, so the owner acts like a bank and carries a note for the balance. Primarily, I bought this property with no money down. I didn't have to qualify for anything. I didn't have to put any cash out there. I didn't have to use any of my credit.

If I could do that in real estate, why couldn't I do that with a business? I started working with that concept. I didn't have my pitch down. I didn't have the right conversations with sellers. Over time I started figuring out what I needed to say, and what I didn't need to say. I had to create a package that made the seller feel comfortable and secure, and then make my part of it more performance-based. So I could literally give the sellers of a corporation a guarantee that I perform and get paid, or if I don't perform I make nothing.

I figured out over time, through experience and trial and error, through the school of hard knocks, how I needed to do it. I can make it risk-free for the sellers, what I call risk reversal. I take all the risk instead of making the seller take the risk. I do the work. I work in conjunction or in partnership with the seller to help them sell their companies for more than their worth, and how to take that company to a new level of growth and profitability. Things really started happening in the '90s when I looked at some of these deals. I've gone back and forth between buying companies to buying real estate to buying companies to buying real estate, to the point where I pretty much do them both.

What I've figured out is that on the real estate side I need to get somebody else to do what I'm doing on the business side. I have my real estate side automated to where I have staff that runs the real estate side. I go out and I find companies alone, or I find companies with some of my partners or my students. We grow those companies,

The EXIT Formula

and now today I am at the point where I have my own private equity company. I own that jointly with a couple of other partners, where we go out and buy, grow, and sell companies. We have a large financial backing and hedge fund money so we can do large deals. We can still do them no money down, or we can put money into deals.

It has grown from being just a one man show to being a much larger organization where it is supported by experts, and as part of our team we have what's called C-level executives. C-level executives are your CEO, CMO, CTO, CIO, your Chief Executive Officer, Chief Marketing Officer, Chief Technology Officer, Chief Information Officer - all those types of C-level executives and consultants. We've been able to build up this whole network that when we go into a company we can tap into our very large network anywhere in the world and bring these people in that can help these companies figure out what do they need to do to grow.

It's not just growth, but we have to figure out what's wrong with the company. We have to really break it down and see what's working in the company and what's not working. We then throw out what's not working, fill the holes on what was working and add new things to take it and make it grow so that ultimately we can resell the company. That's where we've gotten, and that is where I am at today...

However, none of this would have ever happened without my mentor or business growth hacking expert.

Chapter 4

Creating Your Sales Team

After you've chosen your business growth hacking expert, you then need to fill the rest of the slots on your team. While most business owners know how to run their business, not many would say they have the expertise to sell a business. Most know that selling a business may be a once-in-a-lifetime activity with its own legal and accounting problems and concerns. This is one area where experience does count.

The business owner knows his business and should understand better than anyone where it has growth potential, the basis for a higher sale price. But to reach this potential you're going to need the very best team you can assemble.

There aren't many professional advisors who understand how to position a sale around the potential value of your business. They tend to put your sale into a conventional framework based on some "industry-standard multiple" and miss the opportunity to assist you in obtaining the maximum value possible for your business. They can be a huge waste of time and even get in the way of getting a deal done, so you need to be very careful about who you choose to assist you in the most important sale of your life.

There is an old adage that buyers follow: "Never pay the other guy for work that you have to do yourself."

That adage limits what you can sell your business for. You see the potential, but the buyer isn't willing to pay for that potential. And potential is a big part of every business' value.

When you work with a business hacker, we can develop that potential.

The EXIT Formula

We may even see some potential that the seller didn't see. We put the resources in place to develop the potential and over the course of twelve to eighteen months we build the profits and expand the business.

After we "hack" your business - realize its potential and grow profits, then we put the business up for sale. Now the buyer is paying for what has been done rather than paying for potential.

Of course you want to include assistance from your current legal and accounting experts, but remember that although they may be great at what they do on a day-to-day basis, they probably have very little experience in how to maximize the value of a business at time of sale. I would suggest that you want to make sure that you not only include advice from your existing counsel but that you also acquire legal and accounting experts whose main focus is helping businesses to be bought and sold.

I am often asked "should I use a business broker or investment banker to help sell my business?" The answer is: it depends on many things, including your understanding of the process of selling a business, whether you have prepared the business to obtain the best offer. Your business growth hacking expert can help you to determine if you need help from other professionals. Even an experienced business owner who has sold several businesses may need an advisor on his team to assist in the negotiations. There is considerable benefit in having an objective, knowledgeable person providing feedback, suggestions and to keep the negotiation process moving forward. This can often be handled by your business growth hacking expert but depending on the industry, he may also advise you to bring in the other members with expertise in particular areas to maximize your sale value.

You should also not discount that the information provided by your team of experts will help you not only to negotiate the best price possible, but accurate information provided in a timely manner to your potential buyer will help them to feel that they have minimized their risk potential. This is a not to be overlooked critical part of any successful sale.

Finally, as the owner you always need to remember that this is your business, and all final decisions are your responsibility. A smart business owner seeks good advice and the best people to support the sale of his business. This will help you to get the best price possible for your business, but remember that the buck stops with you.

Staffing Your Team

Here is a short list of some of the potential advisors that you might want to include on your team:

- Key members of your management staff
- Your business growth hacking expert
- Mergers and acquisition company or investment banker
- Your current attorney
- Attorney specializing in business sales
- Your current CPA
- A tax specialist specializing in business sales
- Information technology expert
- Business appraiser
- Insurance agent
- Current lenders

This is just a basic list and should not be considered all-inclusive. Not every sale of a business will require the use of all of these experts. Depending on the industry and type of business you may require additional specialists. You should make your selections of whom to place on your team based on your discussions with your business growth hacking expert and other trusted advisors.

Chapter 5

Methods of Selling Your Business

When you decide to sell your business, it is one of the biggest decisions you will have to make. There are several paths you can take, and they are based on how quickly you want to sell and the price that you are willing to accept for your company. Once you know these objectives and others that are important to you, it's time for you to choose the type of sale that will best fit your needs. The sales path you choose is critical to seeing that your most important needs are met.

There are four levels of buyers for most companies. When a business is sold, it has to be valued so people know what they are paying for. Sometimes companies are sold because of their technology, patents, distribution systems, competing products, cash flow, buyer's lists, and a whole lot more. When they are sold, they are generally sold for a multiple. What I mean is that a company can be sold for a multiple of the net profit or sometimes a multiple of the gross revenue. I prefer to look at a business based on the net revenue (profit) because I want a business that can make a profit in the future.

So, let's start with the smallest buyer first. These are:
1. Sell to an Existing Partner
2. Sell to Family Member(s)
3. Sell to a Key Employee
4. Sell to an Individual in an Arm's Length Transaction
5. Sell to a Competitor or Another Business
6. Sell to Employees
7. Liquidate Your Business

This first group is typically a buyer's market. They will typically pay 1-

3 times the net. However, this is usually not the group you want to sell to if maximizing the value of your company is your goal.

The next group is private equity companies. They are typically looking for larger deals. Private equity companies will typically pay 3-6 times the net. With both individual buyers and private equity groups, they will buy companies with seller financing of 40-100% of the purchase price. Individual buyers typically sell to private equity groups.

One short anecdote to illustrate the pitfalls of dealing with private equity buyers.

We know one very successful Chicago based PE firm that looked at seventy deals in 2014 and did one deal. (I say successful, because they have a well paid staff and happy investors who get a good return on their investments.)

That meant that 69 sellers got their hopes up, spent many hours answering due diligence questions, and not working with more realistic buyers.

The one successful seller sold at a price that supported those sixty-nine unsuccessful deals while making the PE Company financially successful.

Would you have wanted to be one of those sixty-nine unsuccessful sellers who wasted their time?

Even worse, would you have wanted to be that one "successful" seller?

Private equity groups sell to the next level, which is merger and acquisition firms. M&A firms have a fixed overhead and will typically only look at deals over $10 million. They generally ignore everything below that because of the cost of doing due diligence. M&A firms buy in the 8-12x range. They look for multiple companies in a similar industry that they can aggregate together to form a single larger corporation so that they can sell the company to the next group of buyers, which are the public companies. M&A firms need to get an aggregate value of $100 million or more so they can sell to Wall Street.

Wall Street (public companies) buys at 15x because they trade at high multiples and every acquisition made at these prices are accretive to them. Additionally, they have an obligation to stockholders and Wall Street analysts explore a pattern for growth, and they can double their money almost instantly. The way they double their money is by selling stock in their corporation to hedge funds, pension plans and private individuals (you) through the stock market at a rate of 15-25x. When we buy publically traded stock, we pay the most for any company that is merged with or purchased by the public company. On average the individual stockholder will take 20 years or more of holding the stock to get a return on investment (ROI) from earnings alone. That leads to a high risk of failure. Granted, we do not have to invest much time and money to manage the way we do, but we still pay the most.

Here is another way of looking at all of these buyers. The small fish gets eaten by the bigger fish, which gets eaten by a bigger fish, which gets eaten by a bigger fish and so on. There is always someone bigger who can buy your company.

Wall Street has an estimated $4-$5 Trillion dollars sitting in reserves so that they can buy companies. That means there is a huge demand for more and more companies. The food chain is constantly needed; today more so than ever before.

The EXIT Formula

Chapter 6

The Realistic Value of Your Business Today

When selling a business, it is critical to get the asking price right. Set it too high, and you won't get any buyer interest. Set it too low, and you'll leave money on the table. So when you set a price for your company make sure that every penny of your company value has been accounted for, while also remaining realistic.

Unfortunately, setting the right asking price for your business is not easy. To determine a price that is fair to you, while still enticing potential buyers, most sellers will want to leverage the expertise of a professional appraiser or business broker. In advance of doing so, however, there are several steps that will help you prepare documentation in the appraisal process and formulate a ballpark estimate of your own:

1. **Estimate the liquidation value of your business by assessing the value of its tangible assets.**

    This works best for more capital-intensive businesses, but is a useful exercise for most small businesses.

    Tip: At the end of the valuation process, compare the business valuation derived from other valuation methodologies to the total value of all tangible assets. If the value of the asset is close to the appropriate asking price for your business, asset sale/liquidation may be a more expedient and cost-effective way to recover the value and exit your business.

2. **Estimate the value of your business using an earnings multiple.**

    Multiples are ratios of business value to key financial indicators, usually revenue and cash flow. Multiples vary according to business type, geography, and a wide host of other factors. As a result, business values typically range from one and four times annual cash flow.

3. **Assemble the necessary financial statements to enable an income-based valuation.**
   - **Organize your financials:**
     Strong business valuations begin with the assembly of formal financial documents for the current year as well as the previous three years. Depending on your bandwidth and accounting skills, you may need a bookkeeper to help you prepare the following essential statements: Income Statement detailing gross revenue, expenses and bottom line profits (or losses).

     Cash Flow Statement showing how money moved in and out of your business, and how business assets changed as a result.

     Balance Sheet showing the value of all tangible assets and liabilities.
   - **Prepare a statement of seller's discretionary earnings:**
     Work with your accountant or bookkeeper to recast your business income into a statement of owner's cash flow or statement of seller's discretionary earnings (SDE). While the income statement reflects the full range of normal and legal deductions, the SDE or owner's cash flow statement presents the full earning power of your business after adding back one-time, non-recurring purchases and discretionary expenses not essential to business operations. It is this full earning power of your business that is, ultimately, of key concern to prospective buyers.
   - **Identify key trends shown by the financial statements:**

Analyze the picture painted by several years of financial statements to understand how your business is growing (or not) in terms of top-line revenue and bottom-line income and what that means for cash flow and seller's discretionary earnings. These trends will typically have a significant impact on your ultimate asking price.

- **Conduct an income-based valuation:**
Most experts agree that this is the best means of valuing a business. Unfortunately, it is also rather complex. As a result, most business owners may want to employ an appraiser who will use the inputs outlined above to derive a business valuation range via this approach. However, by assembling the financial statements and looking at the financial trends, you will be able to better understand, assess and be comfortable with the resulting valuation.

The EXIT Formula

Chapter 7

Methods to Increase the Value of Your Business

Before we get into how to grow your business, we need to first look at where the business is today. What I mean is that you need to look at your company very hard and be honest:
- Are you stuck?
- Have you reached a plateau in your business regarding sales and profits?
- Would you like to sell your company for more than it's worth today?
- Do you know your company can be so much larger and profitable, but you just don't know how to get there?
- Do you want out?
- Would you take a smaller piece of a bigger pie later?

Our firm has helped companies all around the world grow their companies and sell them for more than they are worth today. The biggest thing we find out with companies that we work with is that they are "stuck." They know their companies should be 10-20 times larger, but they do not know for sure how to get there.

The Secret Sauce For Your Business

There is a secret sauce to creating a multi-million dollar company. In fact, I have broken it down into 11 key elements needed to have a million dollar business:

1) *Strategy.* You need a strategy for getting from point A to point B.
2) *WOW experience.* You need customers to say "wow" about your brand, your product or your service.

The EXIT Formula

3) *Marketing.* If you do not have good marketing, you will never bring enough buyers in the door growing the company to any significant size.
4) *Selling.* Your company needs to know how to sell. They need to find their core product and complimentary products that generate the most profit with the least amount of work.
5) *Negotiating.* This is a critical skill for a company that is establishing new vendor and supplier relationships. Also needed if you are going to leverage yours and other company's relational capital to gain access to products, systems, distribution networks, capital and brands that you cannot build or access on your own.
6) *Management.* It is always said that great companies come down to great management. If you are the key person in your company (we call you an owner/operator) this will become a huge challenge in order to sell your company to the next level buyer because you are the company. You need to transition yourself out of the owner/operator role and move to more of the chairman of the board roll. Your management team will transfer to the new owner. In most case, you will not.
7) *Innovation.* Do you have the ability to innovate quickly? Can you come up with new products or systems that will allow you to stay competitive in the marketplace?
8) *Delegation.* This is very hard for most owner/operators. They just don't want to let go of control, and they think that no one will do the job as well as he or she can. This means the owner/operator is stuck in their business. Realizing others can do the job and then letting them do the job is critical to growth.
9) *Technology.* What current technology are you using in your company today that allows you to stay competitive?
10) *Systems.* Having the right systems in place means that you

have a sellable company. With the right systems, your company is not dependent on any single person to stay profitable or grow. Systems are critical to growth.
11) *Follow-up and follow through.* Sounds simple, but this is where many companies lose a lot of sales, additional sales, continuity, and repeat sales. Many companies say they are good at it but when a third party comes in and looks at what is in place, the holes in the process become very apparent.

What the 11 elements above mean is if you can implement those 11 elements in you company, you now have a sellable company, a company positioned for growth. Leave any of these elements out of the mix and your company is not running the way it should or could. Do you see any of the above elements that are missing or could be improved in your company? I am sure you do. Otherwise you would not be reading this book.

Where Most Companies Get It Wrong

Most companies think they need capital to grow the company and increase sales. They believe that with more capital they can buy systems that will increase sales. Then they can hire the right people to manage those systems and they will be able to implement their marketing strategies to get the sales they want.

In reality, most companies, unfortunately, go about their business in reverse order. They think capital will solve the problem and allow them to build the right systems which they can then hire the right people to run who will then implement the right marketing strategies to fix the company. In every company we have bought or partnered with we found they were stuck in at least one, if not all, four areas.

The EXIT Formula

Here is how we look at growing a company so that it can be sold for more than it is worth today:
1) Lack of marketing - #1 killer of small business growth.
2) Lack of talent – Top people usually work for companies that are growing.
3) Lack of systems – This usually comes with good people – Crucial to scale.
4) Lack of capital – To fund only growth after 1, 2, & 3 are addressed.

(These important steps will be explained in depth in chapters 8 through 11.)

We look at the company in a totally different way. While most companies go in reverse order of the above, we fix things in the company as listed above. For instance, most business owners think they need capital to grow their company. When in fact if they fix their marketing it will drive more leads into the business. They then need the right talent to handle the marketing and manage the systems to automate the business and make it grow. By taking care of numbers 1, 2, and 3, it frees up the capital that the owner thinks is needed to grow the company.

The 3 x 3 Matrix

If you implement these ways of growing a business, you will then be able to skyrocket your company's value. I know you are going to absolutely love the math. It's not magic. It's not made up math. It is simple and provable. So let's take a look:

> If a company's profits are $1,000 a day…
> With 3 times more customers, that equals $3,000 a day
> With 3 times the profit per sale, that equals $9,000 a day

The EXIT Formula

With 3 times frequency, that equals $27,000 a day

So if we look at the original version of the company making $1,000 a day, then that equals $365,000 for the year. However, if we triple the customers and we triple the profit per sale and we triple the frequency of the purchase that means the company has gone from a gross sales of $365,000 to $9,885,000! Don't believe me? Just pull out a calculator and do the math yourself. It's shocking!

Now let me give you an even bigger shocker. Let's say you owned the original company doing $365,000 a year in sales. We bought it for 1x the gross sales (that is pretty common for smaller companies). We then turned around and implemented these strategies to grow the company. We put our teams into place to make it happen. Now we want to sell it just 24 months later. Let's also assume I sell it for the same multiple of 1x (because we have increased the business dramatically it will sell for around 3x in reality). We would turn around and sell the company we bought from you for $9,855,000. That's a pretty good return on our investment.

Moreover, we are just getting started!

However, let's say we partnered with you to grow the company and we just did a 50-50 split. Now let's look at your choices. You could keep 100% of the $365,000 sale price if you sold it outright, or you could get half of the $9,855,000 ($4,927,500) by partnering with us. Which would you choose? Would you delay the sale of your company just a short 2-3 years for an extra $4,000,000+?

The above example is what I mean when I ask you if you would take a smaller piece of a bigger pie later. For most people it is a pretty simple answer because our results are proven and predictable.

The EXIT Formula

Chapter 8

Lack of Marketing Can Kill Your Business Growth

Let's start with area number one, marketing. Marketing is the lifeblood of the company. Most closely held companies are too busy to do the marketing properly or the owner is the person who does it. Even worse, they assign it to someone else who does not have the background on how to implement a great (not just good) marketing strategy in the niche that you are in.

So most business owners only see the following options:
1) Learn it yourself – in a couple of years you could be pretty good.
2) Hire it out – Real marketing strategists NEVER work for a paycheck.
3) Partner - The ONLY real option for most businesses.

There are only 3 ways to grow a company. This will take a few minutes to go over, but, if you get this part it will have an immediate impact on your business.

The first method is to Get More Customers. When we partner with companies or buy them, we implement 34 different customer acquisition strategies so that we can achieve hyper growth and triple the profit of the company in about 12-18 months. Here are a few of the strategies we use:
- Bounce Back Offers
- Channels like Amazon, Sears.com, Overstock and NewEgg
- YouTube Marketing
- LinkedIn & Meetup

The EXIT Formula

- Power Referrals
- Trade Publications
- Mobile Marketing
- Trade Show Marketing
- Joint Ventures
- Facebook Ads
- Direct Mail Postcards
- Groupon
- Google AdWords
- Search Engine Optimization
- Social Media Marketing

Most companies don't even implement a fraction of the above. By applying all 34 techniques, we can triple the number of customers in just a short 90 days or less.

The second method is to Increase the Profit per Sale. When we step in with a company we look at three ways to increase the profit per sale:

1) Immediate Upselling - Do You Want Fries with that? (McDonalds).
2) Cross Selling - People who bought (blank) also liked... (Amazon).
3) Bundling - You can get Phone, Cable & Internet... (Comcast).

When we increase the profit per sale, then that means we have the ability to outspend everyone else in our niche to acquire a customer. Because of that, no one can compete with us, and that is why we help our partners to dominate his or her market very quickly and then sell their company for a whole lot more than it's worth today.

You need to be maximizing all of your sale profits. Let me explain what I mean. You need a profit maximizer. Moreover, profit maximisers are simple. All the money comes in here. This is what's all underneath the iceberg.

So I am going to give you a couple of examples. These are what other people call upsells, cross-sells, bundles, things like that. There are a number of these. We have tons more than the examples I can give you here that we used for different partners. However, these are some of the bigger ones, and this will give you a general idea of what's going on.

Let's talk fast food. You do not have to eat it, but you better understand it. I want to use the best in the world, and that is McDonalds. Therefore, McDonalds uses upsells very, very effectively. McDonalds Corporation spends a $1.91 to get somebody to drive through the window at McDonalds. Their average hamburger sells for $2.08. So what is that? That is a $.17 profit. So they make $0.17 per customer that drives through the drive through. But check this out. If you buy the fries and the Coke for another $1.77, they make a $1.38 clear profit. Why? Because they've already paid the cost to acquire the customer. It is already absorbed in the hamburger. The upsell, the fries and then not counting the apple pie, not counting the biggie size, not counting all that stuff. Have you noticed how hard it is now to go to McDonalds and just buy a hamburger? It is next to impossible. They make the value proposition so stupid that you end up buying the big package. If you buy the burger and the Coke, it is the same price as buying the burger and the Coke and the fries.

Think about that for a minute. McDonald's makes ten times more money with the upsells. Imagine making ten times more profit on every sale you make. McDonalds does that.

Cable uses a different method which is called bundling or bundles. So

The EXIT Formula

cable offers are like this: get your phone, your Internet and your TV all for $99 a month. How much is my cable? How much is my phone? How much is my TV? It's all $99 a month. So they do a couple of things with that. One, they raise the ticket to get their profitability up very, very high because the truth is when they're running the cable into your home, it costs them zero additional dollars to deliver Internet service and telephone service to you. I think it's like $1 a month or $0.50 a month for them to deliver the telephone service.

So think of that. The cable is $39, the TV and the Internet together is $99, guess what? 100% pure profit. They're attracting the customer. Advertising will get you to buy their cable services and everything else. Just pure profit.

This is exactly what our private equity firm does. We dig deep into a business and find all those little things the owner has not thought of and create magic by maximizing profits. We have had many companies that we partnered with where parts of the business were running smooth as silk. They were happy. And yet the profit maximizer is just sitting there and maybe they're not offering it or they're not offering it in a different sequence or it's not quite positioned right. Sometimes people have things bundled with the core sale that only complicates the core sales. They would remove it from the core sale and sell this for less money. They could upsell that item and have a lot of more customers come in.

Now let's talk about a cross sale. Let me explain by using Amazon as an example. If you ever bought anything on Amazon, which I bet most of you have, you've seen this line: "Most customers who bought this also bought this." Or "Amazon customers who bought this digital camera also bought this tripod and this SD card and this camera case."

The EXIT Formula

This is another way to increase your profit. 20% to 30% of the people who buy the camera will buy some accessories. Now Amazon spends a lot of money to get a customer to come to the website to buy that camera. So a lot of the profit they made on the camera got eaten up in marketing costs, immediate costs, operations, warehouses, etc. The money they make selling those additional products, whatever their gross profit is, is mostly pure profit. They don't spend anything on extra marketing. It's just a ticket add on.

Starbucks uses another feature called a slack adjuster. Let's say you go into the store for a cup of coffee, which will cost you anywhere from $4 to $7. While you are standing in line you see pastries, music, and Espresso and Cappuccino machines. You've walked in the door, so they already have you as a customer. Now you buy a $14 cd and a muffin for $5. That is a small upsell. While you are in line enjoying the smell of the coffee being brewed and the music over the sound system, you start looking at the Espresso machines. Some of their customers obviously buy these machines. Starbucks would not waste that floor space with a product that does not sell. I was having a private lunch with the CEO of Starbucks, Howard Shultz, talking about business and charities and I asked him how many of those machines he sold each month. He told me he could not disclose the exact numbers (that was confidential) but he said the sale was almost all profit to the store.

So how many cups of coffee do you have to sell to equal one Espresso machine? You have to sell a lot. If you can figure out what the slack adjuster is in your business, it could completely change the economics of what you do. Oh yeah, on a side note. Guess which company sells the most CD's in America right now? You guessed right… Starbucks. All because the customer is already in the door.

The EXIT Formula

There are other companies that use these profit maximizers. More than you know. Let's look at another one. Let's look at Best Buy. If you say the core sale at Best Buy is whatever it is you are buying, the electronics you're buying, then stop here. BestBuy makes no money at all. They sell all of their electronics at pure cost plus overhead. They make zero dollars profit. I know you're thinking that can't be right. They can't stay in business that way. Well, have you noticed that every time you go to the checkout counter they always offer you an insurance plan on the product you just purchased? The only way Best Buy makes money is right when they sell you a warranty, or they sell geek squad service. That is the only way they make money. They give away the electronics. And that's the reason their prices are so much lower than everybody else and that's why they are the largest electronics dealer in the world.

Sneaky, but effective. So what business is Best Buy in? They are in the insurance business.

See why we typically TRIPLE transaction profits in 90 days or less?

The 3rd technique used to grow a company is the increase in the frequency of the purchase. We leverage these four big methods of increasing the frequency with which your customers buy from you:

1) Implement Constant Contact with the customer. This can include, but is not limited to Direct mail, Email, Newsletter, Phone, TXT message, Social Media & Retargeting.
2) Implement Loyalty Programs. This includes such things as VIP promotions, Frequency discounts, free merchandise, and incentivized referrals.
3) Create Continuity Billing. This includes adding auto-billing solutions. This is the VERY best of all methods to increase

frequency of the purchase.
4) Create Line Extensions. Sell more of what our customers often buy via joint ventures.

Do you see why we typically TRIPLE how often customers come back to a business?

The EXIT Formula

Chapter 9

Talented People Work For Growing Companies

As we talk about partners for a few minutes, I want you to keep in mind that having partners does not mean that they are going to do all of the work for you. Even when I partner with companies where we get equity, I don't do everything. Some of things people get access to are my connections and relational capital.

So let's dig in and talk about how to find partners; that's what everybody wanted to know. How do I find people to fund my ideas, to do business with me? This doesn't just apply to real estate or start-up companies. It applies to any business, any joint ventures. I used to be taught "Fake it until you make it. Fake it until you make it. Fake it until you make it." You don't need to fake it. People see right through you when you fake it. You need to act like you belong. You're reading this book; you're in good hands with me. It takes one person, one deal and one opportunity to change your life. I am sincere when I want to do this. I want to help you take your life and your business to the next level. I want to be that one person, whether you are starting out or you are super experienced because that is what is going to make the difference in the market today.

The quickest way to get to the heart of a millionaire is to add value to what is most important to them and their business. Let me repeat that: *the quickest way to get to the heart of a millionaire is to add value to what is most important to them or their business.* To be a successful networker you have to put yourself in the shoes of the people you're going to do business with, so you want to Google the top ten nicest golf courses and you want to memorize them. So when you are talking to somebody who is a golfer, say "hey, have you played at Pebble

The EXIT Formula

Beach? Have you played at Trump National? Have you played at St. Andrews? Have you played at Torrey Pines?" And they might say "No, but I've always wanted to. How about you?" Then you can tell them "My handicap prevents me from playing." However, broke people don't know about these things. I just started learning about polo. I do not know anything about polo. I have no intention of playing polo. All I know is that the average person playing polo makes over $350,000 a year.

Did you know that if you earn $388,000 a year, you're in the top 1% income earning in this country? $388,000 in the next 12 months and you wake up in the top 1%. Isn't that crazy? That is not all that high and that's very achievable for most people to get to if they do it correctly.

You don't need to fake it until you make it. Act like you belong. Playing golf is not about doing business, it's about building relationships. You build that relationship and then at the end of the day you say "You know what? We should really work together." Nobody pitches their idea on the golf course.

Pick up an issue of the Forbes 400. Every single person I know picks up an issue of the Forbes 400. Study these people and how they got to where they are today. Read the Wall Street Journal every day. There was a recent article about Yahoo and the fact that they fired their CEO and how it impacted their business. I'm not in the internet business per se, but it's interesting to learn about what boards are looking for, mergers and acquisitions, and the futures and takeovers. You want to expand your horizon. That is a very important part of success in the market today.

Compliments will get you everywhere; corniness will get you nowhere.

The EXIT Formula

Don't go to people and say "Hey, I'd like to make a win/win." That's just amateur. How many successful people do you know might go up to people and say "Hey, let's make it a win/win?" Negotiation is not about win/win; it's about two parties willing to walk away satisfied. Would you agree with that?

Here is step by step how to find partners in your warm markets:
- Step One: Make a list of everyone you know or have a relationship with.
- Step Two: Rate them A, B, C or D on the basis and likelihood that they will know someone that can help your business. Focus on the A's first, and then the B's, then the C's, but it's important to look at all your relationships.
- Step Three: Call your list and build a relationship with them. Sometimes you haven't talked to them in years or in months, but make the conversation 90% about them, 10% you. Ask them what they're looking for. You always want to add value to other people's business.
- Step Four: Call them back seven days later. Not ten days, not three days, but seven days exactly. If there is something that you can do to add value, pitch it. Once you've made it all about them you can now ask: "By the way, do you know someone that can introduce me to this type of person? Do you know a successful investor?" Then you can ask them to make an introduction. This works very effectively, which brings us then to step number five.
- Step Five: Track every introduction and multi-millionaire relationship. That way you will get a better target of your successful, as well as your unprofitable relationships.
- Step Six: Always make sure you add value to the other person first. The more you give, the more you get. It's always better

when someone asks you for something than when you ask them. Value added propositions.
- Step Seven: Follow-up and follow through. 80% of the deals I've done, 80% of relationships I forged were a result of follow-up and follow through. It's a matter of being persistent and showing value to the other person. It's crucial to making the relationship work, then monetize, then follow up and follow through.
- Step Eight: Understand that not everybody will say "yes." In fact, I expect most people to say "no," but it's that one "yes" that is going to make an entire difference—one person, one deal and one opportunity.

There is a secret to networking with the wealthy. Write these down, pin them up on your bulletin board, and make them your mantra:

1. **Influence the influential.** Sales letters and brochures do not work with people that are wealthy. You cannot send them a proposal; they just don't read it anymore because it just sounds like everybody else. That's an interesting concept that people don't understand in the marketplace. People just don't get it. They go in and they just assume. You know what happens when they assume? It just doesn't work out. It is more important to have that relationship. You want to tap their network and get an introduction. It's not networking with the wealthy, its being in that circle of influence that makes a huge difference in today's marketplace. The more networking you do, the higher probability there will be an overlap.
2. **Make yourself valuable to the wealthy.** You are a problem solver, an information provider, an expert, a moneymaker. These are traits that the wealthy admire.
3. **Nothing is for free.** Make yourself clear. A lot of people say

"Oh, I'll do it for free. I'll follow you around." Everyone knows there is nothing for free. You said, "Listen, if I do this, I would like this." Or just say, "I'm doing this and later on we'll do that." People know that things are not done for free, so that's an important thing in today's market economy.

The EXIT Formula

Chapter 10

Systemizing Your Business

Frustrated With Your Business Results?

Even a well-run business experiences times when things are not running smoothly. Your results depend on how you deal with these situations. If you are feeling frustrated with your business, it is time to sit down and take a good look at certain areas.

Do you find that you just don't have enough time on your hands to accomplish all of your tasks? Or you may find that you are constantly interrupted and never get anything achieved. Or do you hire new people to help, only to spend too much time training and fixing their mistakes?

All of these things can easily be improved by using business systemization methods. There are reasons why you are feeling frustrated, and these come down to a few basic things:

1. You may be causing your own frustration by not allowing others to help and support you. Don't try to run a one man business because it doesn't always work.
2. It is possible that the systems you do have in place are not working. They could be outdated or new staff members are unaware that they exist.
3. If you find that your customers are always coming to you with support issues, do they even know that you have a support desk? If so, then you are really causing your own frustration. Start informing your customers of the correct procedure for submitting a support ticket.

The EXIT Formula

If your problems are centered on finding good staff members, it is possible that your training procedures are not working. Instead of trying to teach someone hands on, think about creating a step by step training manual. Then when you do hire someone new, they can refer to this manual after their initial training period is finished.

If time is your major frustration, start looking at which tasks could be handed off to an assistant. If you are constantly frustrated, this is going to affect your business dealings and possibly rub off on to your customers.

One of the biggest objections to not setting up systems or hiring help is because of the cost. Instead of thinking that you don't have X amount of dollars for hiring someone, think about how valuable the time saved would be to you. You would be much better off to hire an assistant for a few hours a week or month to help free up your time, and save your sanity.

Once you experience the results and free up your time, you can easily hire more help as needed.

What is Business Systemization?

When running your business, do you use any type of system or process that can help you run your business more smoothly? If not, use these tips to help you become more efficient and run a more profitable business.

Business systematization applies to any system that can make your life easier. Think about what types of tasks you do on a regular basis. Can these be systemized in some way?

Let's look at a few examples:

- Email - If you mail your list or send out a newsletter regularly, using a template can really speed things up for you. Having a system in place such as an autoresponder service can also be helpful. They have templates that you can use, or you can create your own custom template. Once you have your template ready to go, it is simply a matter of adding your content and hitting the send button.
- Products - If you sell similar products again and again you can use templates to help you with the actual creation process, as well as the sales process. If you have an effective sales funnel in place, try to systemize as much of it as possible. This way you can easily replicate the process and just fine tune it to each individual product.
- Customer Service and Support – Hire someone to take care of your customers. Your time is better spent making money.
- Daily Tasks - Just think about any task that you do on a daily or weekly basis that takes up your time, such as posting to your social media accounts. Look for a way to systemize the process.

Some of the best systemized business models are McDonalds, Starbucks and in Canada, Tim Horton's. They have all developed systems and processes that allow new business owners to quickly learn how to run their own franchise successfully.

Do you have a systems manual you could hand over to someone that would explain how to run your business? If not, then you should really start implementing one now. What if you run a small business and you get sick or hurt... how would your business survive? You don't want to run the risk of losing it just because you can't work. Instead, if you have a system in place, someone else can easily take over for you at any time.

The EXIT Formula

If you haven't paid much attention to business systemization, hopefully this will open your eyes to the importance of it.

Can Your Business Run Without You?

Can you honestly say that you could leave your business for a few weeks or months and it would run without you? Unfortunately, most small business owners cannot answer 'yes' to this question. However, there is a solution to this and it is not as hard to implement as you might think.

Systemizing your business is the best way to free up your time, and it enables you to leave your business alone if necessary. Now this may sound like a complicated task, so let's break it down.

For at least one month you want to write down all the tasks that you do. Include everything from answering emails, posting to Facebook, answering calls, writing articles and marketing your business. List it all!

Now go back down your list and start to see which items or tasks you could either hand off to an assistant or which could use an automation tool. For those tasks that could be automated, why haven't you done so already?

One easy task which you can use an automation tool for is scheduling posts to your social sites. There are lots of tools that can do this for you. All you have to do is spend a few hours each month setting it up. Then you don't have to worry about posting to these sites for weeks at a time.

For the list of tasks that you could hand off to an assistant, do you have training manuals to help show them what to do? If not, create them first before hiring someone.

The EXIT Formula

Go through all of the required steps until you have every detail covered. When you do hire someone all you have to do is to give them a quick overview of what is required. Then you can feel comfortable that your training manual will help them accomplish the task to your specifications.

Ideally you should end up with a system in place for every aspect of your business. This would include having a training or instruction manual for:
- How to send an email or newsletter to your list of customers.
- How to update your website or who to contact.
- How to order new products.
- How to add a new product to your website.
- How to hire an assistant if your current one becomes sick.
- Who to order graphics from.

Of course, the list goes on from here and will vary depending upon your business. Your end result when it comes to systemizing your business is one that allows you to hand off the day to day running of it to someone else without any worries.

Stop Being a One Man Show

Are you still trying to run your business as a one man show? If so, it is time to stop. Don't you want to free up your time, save money and just sleep better at night? Let's look at how you can accomplish these things:

Your first step is to stop trying to do everything yourself. If you are marketing your business, doing your books, dealing with customer support and creating or ordering products, then you are totally overworked. So by this point you probably aren't even enjoying your

The EXIT Formula

business that much.

Instead, you want to start documenting everything that you do on a daily basis. Then take a step back and see how certain areas can be improved. For example, you may send out daily emails to your list. While this is a great marketing tactic, it can eat into your time. Instead of writing one new email each day, sit down and plan out your emails for an entire week. Then load them up in your autoresponder and schedule them to go out. Do this on a Monday and you have freed up your time from this task for an entire week.

Next you want to start creating goals for your business. As well as writing out your goals, write out what your strengths and weaknesses are. Take a look at your weaknesses and make a point of handing this off to someone else. Why waste 6 hours of your time trying to create graphics when a professional can do it in 2 hours?

Start creating procedure sheets or manuals for everything you do.

These can be as simple as a one page document, or as complex as a 500 page manual. The advantage to this is that you can hand off these documents to someone new, and they can easily take over.

Create templates for things like how to set up a new customer account, or how to deposit money into the bank. Again, these can be given to an employee who can easily follow your instructions. This frees up your time and takes a lot of stress off of you. However, if you end up with long winded templates or manuals, try to refine them into shorter steps. While you may have initially written the manual, have the person who is performing the task tweak it. What you explained in 5 steps may be cut down to 2.

Once you have systems in place then you need to let go and hire some help. This could be an actual employee who comes in every day. Or you could hire a virtual assistant that works remotely for you. A good example of this is hiring someone to manage your customer service desk. They work for 2 hours each day and answer support tickets.

So are you ready to stop being a one man show and start systemizing your business so that it can run without you for a while?

Creating Your Business Systems

Let's take a look at how you can easily create systems and processes to systemize your business. One thing to keep in mind is that there is no 'one size fits all' when it comes to business systemization. Instead, you have to work on creating ones that suit your own business and the methods you use.

Creating Manuals
Having manuals for each area of your business can really help you stay productive. If you have an instruction manual for a particular machine, when a new person takes over, they can quickly get up to speed.

Start this process now by getting staff members to document all the steps needed to perform a certain task. Once complete, test this out by having someone new see if they can complete the task by following the manual. Fine tune it until this process works.

Using Tools and Services
If you find yourself wearing too many hats and running out of time in your business, you are in serious need of some help. Try looking for tools that can help you free up your time and ultimately increase your profits.

Any type of repetitive task can be automated. Are you still sending out emails by hand? Why not use an autoresponder service to help you with this?

If you spend an hour a day posting messages on your social pages, then use a tool that can help you automate this. Hootsuite is a good example. You can easily use these tools to send out messages for weeks at a time. You spend time setting it up once a month and then don't have to bother with it again.

Another idea is to hire the help of a virtual assistant. They can easily take over repetitive tasks from you. They could learn how to answer your customer service emails. They could post your content to your Facebook business page for you and more. Yes, it does take time to train them, but once you have done this step you are freeing up a good chunk of your time.

Hopefully by now you are beginning to see that systemizing your business isn't as difficult as you may have thought. Start by systemizing one area and go from there. Before you know it, you will have more time and energy to direct towards more important areas of your business.

Developing Your Systemized Training Manuals

One of the easiest systems for any business to put in place is by creating training manuals. These don't have to be huge by any standard, but they do need to be well written and easy to understand. Plus, they must be kept up to date; if not, they are useless.

A good training manual is one that teaches the reader how to follow a process from the beginning to the end. No step should be left out, and it should include tips on rectifying issues should they occur.

The EXIT Formula

The best way to write or develop your training manual is to document each step. This will take time and effort, and no doubt, small steps will be left out. This will be because the person doing the task is so familiar with it that they will leave out obvious things. The whole trick to a good training manual is to not leave out those small items. Once the first draft of the manual has been prepared, hand it over to someone who is unfamiliar with the process. Then see if they can complete the task without any help. If they can, your manual is finished. If not, go back in and make revisions until anyone can do the process.

A customer service training manual is an excellent business tool to have. This way you can ensure that all of your customer service representatives are following the same procedures. All support tickets or customer calls will be handled professionally and have that company stamp to them.

The biggest issue with training manuals is keeping them up to date. If your company is large, then you can easily assign one person this responsibility. On average, each training manual should be reviewed about every six months. If new tools or software are used, then add updating manuals to one of your templates.

Templates are an easy way to systemize your business. You can use templates for all kinds of tasks including emails, newsletters, business letters, sales letters, short processes and more.

A template is a fill in the blanks type of document that just needs updating. It is a great tool to use for writing sales messages or product releases. Plus they can be handed to anyone with simple instructions on how to complete them.

Creating and developing new training manuals can be time-consuming. Once they are in place, however, you will appreciate their full benefit. Your company will be more streamlined than ever before.

Grow Your Business By Systemizing

Is your business stuck in a rut and not growing as fast as you had hoped for, or not at all? If you answered "yes" then your business could probably do with some systemizing.

Not sure what business systemizing is? It is a process of taking your daily activities and tasks and streamlining them. Think of your business as a large shelf with small racks and ladders funneling into it. These small ladders are your systems that feed your entire business.

The best way to grow your business is by increasing your productivity. If you create online products, for example, the more products you have for sale increases your profitability. Not having streamlined processes can really eat into your time and hampers your productivity.

Before you can start systemizing and growing your business, you need to have a vision for your business. Do you know what your goals are and where you are headed? If not, take some time to work this out first.

Now start looking at what obstacles you have. Identify all those things that you feel are holding you back from growing your business. Are you working for clients? Does customer service eat up all of your time? Make a list of everything, as these will become your first targets when it comes to systemizing your business.

Basically any task can be turned into a system, but you should focus on those things that you either don't like doing or have difficulty with. Look for repetitive tasks that have to be done but are time-consuming. This might include things such as:

- Preparing invoices
- Preparing quotes
- Sending out emails
- Bookkeeping tasks
- Proofreading and editing
- Writing blog posts

Each one of these items can be turned into a procedure, either by creating a 'how to' document or by writing a longer training manual for it. Remember to include all necessary steps in your manual. Try to write it from the perspective of teaching someone who is totally unfamiliar with the process. It may even help to create videos or take screen shots of certain parts of the system.

Once you have created these documents, you are now ready to hire people to help you run your business. This leaves you time to work on things such as marketing, creating new products, and attracting new customers, which in turn will help grow your business and your profits.

Systemizing Your Main Business Challenges

A well-run business is one that is streamlined and developed to take care of your major business challenges. All businesses, at some point, have a challenge. Your business may be too big to be run alone anymore, or you may need to use new software to keep it running smoothly.

Let's look at a business model that is not systemized first:

As the business owner, you are feeling frustrated and overwhelmed. You are working crazy hours and still don't manage to get everything done. You hire people to help you but don't have time to train them properly. This results in more mistakes and errors that you now have to fix.

Next let's look at what systemizing your business means:

Systemizing your business entails you looking at what systems you currently use, what works and what needs to be improved upon. Then you have to create systems that work so that they all fit together to form one larger system.

The end result is that you have one main business system that has smaller systems which feed into it. While each component can work independently, they all rely on each other in order for your business to work and function smoothly.

Now, let's identify your challenges:

Your challenge areas are simply those that require the most time and effort from you. These are the ones that you may often consider to be a real pain! Or those things that give you sleepless nights. Identify these areas and make a list of them. Then start creating and using systems to improve them.

Here's a smoothly run and systemized business:
- Training manuals in place for each task.
- Automated tools used as much as possible.
- Customers who know where to go for support and help.
- Employees who understand what their job function is and how to do it.
- A company that is open to ideas and suggestions.

This can all be accomplished by carefully taking the time to plan out and recognize all of your tasks. The best way to accomplish this is to keep track of every detail of your business. This includes noting down what your daily, weekly, bi-weekly, monthly and yearly tasks are. Then working on implementing systems, so no area is left out. By doing this, you will find that your biggest challenges and frustrations are now more streamlined. You have more time and effort to run your business as a business owner, and not as an overworked employee!

Tips for Systemizing Your Business

Documenting your procedures is one of the best ways to systemize your business. These documents should be as detailed as possible, with no step left out. Over time they will be fine-tuned and updated as your systems change and evolve.

Having operating or training manuals in place can help the process of training any new employee much easier. It can also help keep employees happy so that they stay with you longer. They know exactly what to do and what is expected of them.

Even a small business, or a one person business should have manuals and procedures in place. Have you ever thought of what you would do if you couldn't run your business for six weeks or more? Training manuals allow you to hand over your business operations at a moment's notice with fewer complications.

Depending upon your systems and procedures, you may find that it can be helpful to create training videos. This is sometimes much faster than writing out long-winded instructions. The advantage of video training is the person can stop and restart the video as necessary. Videos are a great tool to use if you use a virtual assistant in your business.

Another great way to systemize your business is by delegating tasks. Yes, we know this can be hard for some people, but if you want your business to grow you have to let some things go. Learn to hand things over to someone else.

Once you have systems in place, you must still remember to monitor them. They will need tweaking and regularly updating. Any time you make a change to one of your systems, remember to update the training manuals accordingly.

Things to monitor include seeing if the tasks are being completed correctly. If you have to constantly fix mistakes, something in your manual is wrong. This could be the user misunderstanding your instructions, or that the instructions themselves were confusing. You should also be open and encourage any team members to offer suggestions to help improve your processes. After all, they are the ones using them.

At the same time, you should be taking advantage of technology and implementing new techniques when appropriate. Software is constantly changing, and there may be a better tool for something that you have been using for years. Be willing to make changes.

If you consistently apply and use these business systemizing tips you will quickly be running an efficient business.

Mistakes to Avoid When Systemizing Your Business

While you may understand the importance of systemizing your business, there are some pitfalls that you want to avoid making:

- Jumping in with no plan - this just has to be one of the worst mistakes you can make. You are totally excited about systemizing your processes, and then you go ahead full steam without any plan. Instead, you need to stop, think and plan first. Then start implementing your systems one step at a time.

- Looking for shortcuts - you can't copy the systems of another business. Each business is run differently, and your systems need to fit your own processes to a tee. You wouldn't expect to use the McDonald's system and run a Starbucks franchise with it.

- Having no manuals in place - as the business owner, you may know how each step of your business works, but nobody else does. This is why you need to create some type of operational manual for each area of your business. Start off by creating training manuals for each job or step of your business. Your end goal is to have enough manuals so that anyone could easily take over any area of your business.

- Processes are not being followed - even if you do have training manuals, are they being used? If your employees are not adhering to your manuals, look for the reason why. They may be out of date, or the employee thinks they have a better way! When systems are followed correctly, they should increase productivity and your profitability.

- Not having clearly defined goals - each system that you have in place should be clearly set out, and it should provide results. While creating training manuals is a good first step, you need to test them out to ensure that they are correct. Plus, when any software or tool is updated, the manual should also be updated.

All of this boils down to not putting enough time, effort and thought into how to systemize your business. As I've mentioned, you can't just copy what another business is doing. However, you can use their ideas and adapt and fine tune them to fit your business.

The EXIT Formula

Before starting any type of business systemization write down all of the systems and tasks that you currently use. Then take one at a time and start developing a way to create a manual for it. Or you can look at tools that could help you automate the entire process.

Chapter 11
Capital Comes In Many Different Forms

There are four types of capital in today's market:
1. *Financial Capital* - That's the money for your deals, your marketing or whatever you spend it on.
2. *Educational Capital* - This is for all types of education, whether it be for school, seminars, coaching or mentoring. I have five coaches. I don't make any business decision unless I bounce it off my coaches.
3. *Social Capital* - The more you give, the more you get. I know a lot of people right now who want to help people, but there is an old expression that you can't help people unless you help yourself first. It's nice to help people, but people don't want help from people who are broke. So you have to be able to help yourself first.
4. *Relational Capital* – Call it relational capital or relationship marketing, but everything comes down to your relationship in today's market economy. You may have the greatest real estate deal, the greatest idea or the greatest product, but if people don't like you they're not going to invest with you and they're not going to buy from you.

Partnering With $$$

So what I want to talk about briefly is how to partner with people that have money. Banks are seldom lending, and they're lending to the people that have money. And how to partner, how to network, how to get them to promote for you, to do business with you.

But most importantly, write this word down, how to infiltrate circles of Influence.

The EXIT Formula

Most people are wondering "why haven't I achieved the success I've wanted to achieve so far?" There are five reasons:

1. **Time management** - People are not very good at managing their time. It's not so much about time management but also energy management. Everyone is focused on to-do lists rather than focused on *to-be* lists. What do I want to be before I can do? But more importantly, you've got to have a stop-doing list. What are the things that you're doing right now that are preventing you from actually going out there and making things happen? That's what we have to change.
2. **Lack of Education** - "I don't know how to do this type of real estate or this type of business or this type of industry." When I don't know something I reach out and find people who do. I'll buy courses, read books, call experts, and find mentors or partners to help me solve my problem.
3. **Lack of Focus** - Don't do 5,000 things 5 times. Do five things 5,000 times. Procrastination is another issue that holds people back. They just don't have a blueprint.
4. **Lack of funds** - This is very much an obvious issue, which can be easily rectified. Therefore, that's what partnerships and Joint Ventures are for.
5. **Fear** - Fear of failure, fear of what other people are going to think, fear of action.

These are the main things that are stopping people from taking their life and their business to the next level. I'm hoping to change that. I am a big believer that if you change your life you're going to create your own economy. Don't worry about the negativity; it's really hard to focus because the news is so negative. But if everybody is doing it, you should do the opposite. I'm not going to sit here and tell you now is the greatest time to get started, because every successful person knows that. And even if it was, we've heard it so many times. This is your time to be unique. This is your time to be different. This is your time to do what nobody else is doing.

90% of your income is going to come from 10% of your relationships. It costs seven times more to get a new partner than it does to work on an existing one.

You have to change your thinking if you're going to grow. Otherwise, you're still thinking the same thoughts you've always had and expecting different results. Oh wait, yeah, they call that insanity!

The EXIT Formula

Chapter 12

Getting More Customers

The first thing to look at is something we call Customer Value Optimization. This goes back to what I mentioned in the beginning about how much you can spend to acquire a new customer. Basically, if you're able and willing to spend the most on acquiring customers, you will win. This process is about Customer Value Optimization. So as we're going forward, take inventory of your own business. What are you currently doing that would fall into one of these categories as we go through the steps? Where you find the hole in your business, that's going to be one of the biggest areas that's holding you back. You want to fill in those holes and you want to optimize and maximize what is here, and we'll talk about that as well.

In short, the sales process looks like this:
- Convince someone they have a problem.
- Convince them you have a solution.
- Get them to trust you enough to buy your product or service.

When dealing in physical products, the value of the product is obvious to the buyer, and the basic sales process is as follows:
1) Customer Searches for Product
2) Your Site Shows Up For That Product
3) Customer Visits Your Site
4) You Sell Them What They Are Looking For

Of course, there is plenty of work involved in appearing where my customers are searching, and there are many factors that go into creating a quality website that is appropriate for your business.

So the first big, big aspect that you will need as a part of the customer value optimization process (and what we do) is what we call the lead magnet. There are a lot of businesses that just aren't using it. However, there are a lot of businesses that are using it, but they don't maximize it as well as they should.

The lead magnet is an opportunity for a customer to raise their hand, for a customer to stand up and say, "I'm a prospect. I'm someone that you should absolutely focus on." What it gives you is the opportunity, once you capture that lead, to market to them over and over and over again. Which anybody who has any sales experience at all will tell you, the vast majority of sales don't occur on the first contact; they occur after the fifth, sixth, seventh, eighth or ninth, depending on the market.

This is also an opportunity to get them to know, like and trust you. So specific to lead magnet, what are some common lead magnets?

A lead magnet is where you get a potential customer to raise their hand and say, "I'm interested in what you're doing." This by itself makes them automatically somewhere between 100 to 300 times more likely to buy whatever it is you're selling in the future versus just knocking on doors down the street randomly or sending a piece of mail through the phone book or calling people at home that have no interest in what you do. So it is a giant tenet to this process.

Different lead magnets, or all lead magnets, are really just an ethical bribe you give to someone to exchange information with. It's a transaction. And largely, it's the first transaction that you'll have with a customer. So you need to make sure it's a good one. So whatever you're giving them in exchange for their contact information, they need to get value from that. It needs to be good. It doesn't have to be big, but it has to be good. It has to be usable. So the first kind of lead magnet that most people give away is information. So a good example is my friend Tony Abrams, who owns an HVAC company and beats his competition by giving away a report on how a lot of HVAC companies scam you. When they come to your house, they don't clean your vents or your furnace properly. They may overcharge for add-ons and sell you things you don't need out of fear. So Tony gave this guide away to people to help them pick a great HVAC company.

Well, guess which HVAC company they picked after they read his guide? Him, right. That's a piece of information. A lot of people do this with free books, with free guides, with free eBooks. You see this all the time online. Free reports, white papers, infographics, and things like that. Pieces of information that you will exchange for contact information because people want that information.

The second thing is free samples. And you see this a lot in the malls around the country. Cosmetic companies do this. They'll give you a free sample, or you go online, and it's like send me a free sample and they get your contact information, a place to send you a sample to. What you're really giving them at that point is not a free sample, it's pre-proof. They want to see if what you've got really works or not. If you're going to be in the sampling process, one of the greatest tripwires in the world was Chick-Fil-A. Chick-Fil-A stood in front of their stores in malls for years and gave away, what? What was their lead magnet? Little pieces of chicken.

These little pieces of chicken on a stick built a billion dollar chicken empire. Chick-Fil-A's model is to give away tons of free chicken because people like the taste and a large percentage of the tasters will buy a meal and come back for more meals later.

Another example of a lead magnet that I am sure you see all the time but don't realize what they are doing is the "price lead magnet." A price lead magnet is where people will give you their personal contact information in return for you giving them the price of a product or getting access to a catalog. Sears, JC Penny, Macy's, and other catalog companies would give you a catalog, but you have to give them your contact info.

Car dealers and Realtors have also started to grab on to this idea. Car dealers have learned that when a customer calls about a car that is on the lot or on a website they don't just give them the information about the price. They get the client to give up some personal information first. The most common thing they ask for is a phone number. They're doing that because they want to get your contact information and have the ability to follow-up with you later on because they know if they're talking to you, their odds of selling you a car with a guy that's not talking to you go up by 10 or 15 times. Realtors do the same thing. They have a sign in the yard with a phone number. When someone calls on the number they ask for your number and will call you back with the price after they look it up. Now they have your contact info. This is smart business practice.

And then the last thing is a small service. This is great for service kinds of businesses. One of my friends is in the real estate business. They do many appraisals on property because they found that people who are about to sell their house want to know what it's worth. So by providing them a mini appraisal as a service, they were able to give them the appraisal, give them the answer to their question and have a better chance of listing the home for sale than if they didn't.

So that's a lead magnet. The general idea here is you just want people to raise their hands, say they're interested in what you're doing, and give you their contact information and permission to market to them in the future. That's it. It's simple and it's easy, but most people skip this process.

And this is another factor; there are a lot of companies that will go out there with a half-hearted effort and will put some type of lead magnet in place but they won't necessarily encourage consumption of that lead magnet or they won't do one of the other things that we'll get to in a little bit. The lead magnet just gets you a shot. If you don't do some of the other things that we're talking about, the results will definitely be "hit and miss."

So think about this. As you surf the web, you might see different blogs and websites where they ask for your name and email, but they don't give you a clear reason as to why you should give them your information. In fact, I have seen many sites that never even ask for your email. That just means that a potential shopper came to the site, left without buying anything and then probably went and bought from a competitor. Just by offering an "ethical bribe" or widget you can get 50% to 70% of people that come to the website to give you their contact information. If you're at a trade show, people give away contact information for drawings. These things are applicable no matter where you're selling, whether you're selling online, in person, from the stage, webinars, tele-seminars - it doesn't matter. The same principles apply.

The Magic of a Tripwire

Remember, people only buy from you after they know you, like you and trust you. If you have a new customer come to your website and they don't know you they might be a little skeptical about buying something from you. Giving them something free that educates them about you and your company is a huge step in the right direction. It

The EXIT Formula

also establishes your credibility. Now we need to combine the Lead Magnet with something called a "Tripwire." I think this is the most largely misunderstood piece of the entire selling process. The big idea here is that a Tripwire sale is just a small, tiny, little sale that turns a person from a prospect into a customer. And that's a magical thing.

When somebody gives you $1, $5 or more, your relationship with the customer instantly changes. Now he is your client and you are his advisor in this particular role. Or he is my customer and I'm his vendor. I automatically have an authority or an expert position because he's paid me money. Once someone has bought something from you, even if it's for a dollar, he's 20 times on average more likely to buy something else from you for way, way more money. Did you hear that? 20x times more likely.

Here is an example of a Tripwire. I was recently on an airplane from Chicago to San Francisco. On the airplane they had a magazine in the back of each seat called Hemispheres, which had articles and ads in it. As I was scrolling through the magazine I noticed an ad for cigars. Now I am not a big cigar smoker, but I like them occasionally with friends. This ad was offering 20 cigars for $19.95. They had a bonus of a small humidor to keep the cigars fresh. They also had a guillotine cigar cutter and a long lasting torch lighter to light the cigars. Wow! All that for $19.95. That's a bargain, since most cigars cost from $8-$40 each. So that's a value of $160-$800, not including the bonuses. If you were a cigar smoker, you would be crazy to pass on this deal.

So the question is "are they making money?" How can they possibly sell all that for only $20 bucks and stay in business? The answer is that the $20 bucks is a loss leader for them. They know that if they get you as a customer they can sell you other things. It turns out this company sells expensive lighters and humidors that cost thousands of dollars.

The EXIT Formula

They know who their client is and that the client will want to protect all of their cigars with a fancy humidor they can impress their friends with. This company is not in the cigar business. They are in the humidor and lighter business.

And the great thing is you can't compete with that offer. The average cigar store down the street can't compete. If they were to give 20 cigars, a humidor, a lighter and a cutter for $19.95, they would go out of business.

Let me bring this back to what I talked about being willing/able to spend more than your competition to acquire a customer. And that's what you have there. The appearance from the outside is that they're going negative and they're losing money to acquire customers, but in reality they've brought in more customers and made more money.

A timelier example is Groupon deals. So at its heart, Groupon is designed to be a tripwire. Now a lot of people don't know how to use Groupon correctly. But the general idea is they give you a coupon worth $25 towards a meal at a local restaurant, you go and get a great meal and you may go back to that restaurant again. You may bring your friends. You may add alcohol. The bill will add up very quickly. And where the restaurant really messed that up, and this is the big lesson -- where the restaurant messed that up was when the customer came in to get a $50 meal with a $25 coupon and they were given a limited menu or rush service. Once that happens, there will not be repeat business.

One of the reasons that Groupon has had such a hard time and why the businesses that have done Groupon deals had such a hard time was because they get this influx of customers and they deliver a poor experience. Not because they want to, but because they are actually overwhelmed by the idea.

Therefore, what I have shared with you so far is more than what 90% of companies out there even do. Getting these concepts makes you so far ahead it's hard to imagine how well you'll do once you get there.

There's never been a harder time to get people to give you money the first time. But on the flip side, there's never been an easier time ever in history to get people to give you money the second time.

If you get to this point in this process and you've delivered value, they'll chase you down to give you their money. People are so happy to find somebody that actually delivers, and that's you.

Is Free Really Better?

The next kind of tripwire is the free trial. I'm going to talk about this because we have to. I don't like free trials. And the reason I don't like them is because I think they instantaneously cast a doubt in the mind of the buyer. Nothing is free. What's the hook? What's the catch? I'd much rather sell them something for $1 or $2 or $3 or $5.

I remember watching Oprah several years ago. She did a little experiment where she brought out white tennis shoes to the audience. She told everyone that there were only the left shoes. She said you could have one for free. Guess what happened? Everyone started pushing and shoving to get one left shoe. Why? Because it was free. She followed that up with another story of how she had a bunch of flowers in her office that were wilting and needed to be thrown out. She left them in the hallway and someone picked them up and took them home because they were free. They did not buy anything; they were just looking for free stuff. I would much rather have a $1 buyer than a bunch of people who gave me their information for a free offer. How about you?

Another example is some initial sales offers that are called "free plus shipping" offers. This kind of offer gives you a product for free, you just pay for shipping. Typically it is for a price of $4.95. That was working before, but now the model has changed around to be a $4.95 product with free shipping. In fact, free shipping as a bonus is very popular and has been known to increase sales as much as 14%.

Tripwires are an important part of your business. This is the one thing that most companies that are struggling just don't have. If you're missing it, you are going to be stalled in your growth forever.

So think about Tripwires you could implement in your business. What do you have in your business today that could be a Tripwire? Take an inventory. What do you have right now that maybe you're giving away that you could actually charge for? What do you have right now that you're selling as a component of something that you're doing that you could deliver that's still a tremendous value, but deliver for less, like Groupon? What do you have that could be a tripwire?

The EXIT Formula

Chapter 13

Finishing the Process Increases Your Bottom Line

For most companies, the sales process is pretty straight forward. Here's a brief overview of what it takes to build a successful business in this space. This can also be used to sell physical products online like several e-commerce companies that I have bought in order to be successful.

Find a product to sell. Your company already has products to sell. What you have to figure out is which products are generating the largest percentage (prefer 80%) of your profit. A lot of companies get hung up on having lots of products to sell. The challenge they run into is that they oftentimes will spend a lot of time selling that 20% of products that do not generate much profit. In fact, they are selling products that should be eliminated from the offering and focus on the profitable ones.

Get a platform from which to sell your products. This step was much more difficult when I started out years ago. Back then we didn't have the one-click Web shopping carts available today. You needed to learn HTML and programming and a variety of other technical skills. Today there is an abundance of out-of-the-box shopping carts like Shopify, BigCommerce, Volusion, etc., which make it easy to build your store. The stores are all pre-built and ready to turn on in five minutes. With these solutions you don't need to know how to code or program or any of that stuff – just sign up for a free trial and list your products. (Note: As I mentioned earlier, you could skip this step and list your products only on channels, but I highly recommend against it.)

Get traffic to your store. Traffic refers to any method of getting those prospective buyers to see your product. There are a number of ways to do this: paid traffic, buyer engines, search engine optimization, social media, etc. The more traffic sources you have the better, because more visitors mean more sales. For testing, simply use the FREE buyer traffic at Amazon, eBay, Sears, and others...

Add value to your market. Now this is the Secret Sauce ... the veritable icing on the cake. Once you have set yourself up with a successful system for making sales, look for ways to add more value for your customers. How can you serve them beyond just delivering their products on time and with good customer service? By answering this question in your marketplace, you will find ways to engage with your customer base beyond the sales process. Doing this builds goodwill and keeps you fresh in their minds, which means the next time they are in the market for products you offer, they will likely return to you instead of buying from a competitor. In other words, customer loyalty depends on the quality of the relationship you build with your consumers. If you ignore them, they'll forget about you, but if you engage them with content they find interesting, they'll remember, and more importantly, become repeat customers.

Value Optimization Process Part II

In the last chapter we spoke about Lead Magnets and Tripwires. The third of five parts is the one that you are familiar with right now. This is your core sale. This is the thing that you're already probably selling or you're planning to sell if you're a start-up. This is the widget. This is the thing you're going to sell. I'm not going to spend a lot of time on this because the truth is you probably already thought this out pretty well. You probably already have a pretty good product and value proposition. But the point is this: by the time you've done those first two things, your lead magnet and tripwire, this becomes automatic.

The EXIT Formula

This is the thing that most people pay for. They'll hire conversion rate optimization specialists. They'll hire sales people. They'll hire all these people to do the heavy lifting that this is. And really, if you can just do the first two, like I said, this becomes automatic.

I'll give you a great example. I have a client that's in the local marketing services business. They help butchers, bakers, candlestick makers, to run pizza restaurants better or to market a bit. And their services are very expensive, about $1,500 a month.

In order to really make money they would have to go out and call on 100 clients and do a presentation to get five clients. So they had about 5% conversion rate at $1,500. I consulted with them to come up with a $20 service to where they will just go out and shoot a little YouTube video, optimize it and put it on YouTube for their client for $20. After they sat through the presentation, almost every client bought the $20 thing. It's like buying a stick of gum at that point. Almost everyone did it because they wanted to see if they could actually perform.

So after they put up the YouTube video, optimized it and got a little press for their business, they went back to them, gave them their results and asked, "Now, would you like to engage our services for $1,500 a month?" 70% of the businesses said, "Yes." That's the difference. If you deliver results in advance, you position yourself so far away nobody can even get near you.

So one of the things you need to remember is that whatever you are selling, when you finally get to the point of presentation, they're already predisposed from all this to buy whatever it is you're selling. They've already had one good transaction for free. They had another good transaction with you (think the YouTube video) for a little bit of money. Now they are willing to go all in.

The EXIT Formula

Now remember if you gave them way more than their money's worth here, they're expecting they're going to get way more than their money's worth with your full service. So they're going to be happy to buy something else from you. As you meet with them or as soon as you give them a presentation, you want to make the big promise. Tell them what's in it for them. Not why you want to make the sale but why they need or want what you're selling.

People have to believe you. That's the number one reason people don't buy whatever you're selling - they just don't believe you. They don't believe it's for them, number one. So you have to make sure the promise is to them because they don't believe what you're selling or they don't believe what you're saying.

Now you've done a lot to build trust with Lead Magnets and Tripwires where most people go in cold, and that's the reason it's so hard to sell. But you still need to remember, they have to believe whatever it is that you're telling them.

Let me give you an example of how to get people to believe in your offer. If you're a personal trainer, you have to, in some cases, help them believe that they can do whatever they need to do. We do with our clients what's known as the Points of Belief audit. So we actually go through their message and they say, okay, you're asking that people believe this and this. And sometimes you're asking them if they believe this about themselves. Sometimes, you're asking if they believe this about the products. Sometimes you're asking if they believe something about society or the world. We are looking for the one Point of Belief.

We've found that the best sales presentation we've ever done was when you asked people to believe one singular thing. If you can get people to believe one thing, it's relatively easy to do. You can spend all your time focusing on that one thing. A lot of people bring out five or six things they want you to believe. They make five or six claims and then spend very little time substantiating those claims, and that's when you lose.

So you need to make them believe. What's the best way to make them believe? Solid, undeniable proof. Nothing is trust-proof. Billy Mays was one of my favorite people before he passed away, and everybody thought Billy Mays was charismatic and a great salesman and all those things and a great copywriter and he was great on camera. And he was all of those things. He was charismatic. But forget all that.

Billy would tell you the reason he sold a lot of stuff is because in every presentation he ever did, there was a wow element. There was a proof element that could not be denied. I remember the flip thing, the weather thing for your feet that he wrapped around his hand and beat his hand with a hammer. He would do all these nutty things that proved a point. You couldn't deny that whatever he was selling worked. It was undeniable.

If you've got a strong proof element, a demonstration of some sort that demonstrates your product really works and does what it says it does, you are 100 times ahead of the ball game.

I remember seeing an ad where this guy drives golf balls through a piece of plywood and says, "Hey, you want to learn how to drive a golf ball harder? Just enter your email address below." There was no copy, no salesmanship. They don't need it. You're seeing a guy standing there whacking golf balls through a solid piece of plywood. It doesn't take long to convince you that this guy hits the ball further than you do.

The EXIT Formula

The next thing you have to look at for your core sale is what we call the "irresistible offer." Your offer needs to be irresistible to the buyer. It's like selling ice to an Eskimo. They just need to believe they have to have it. You want to tell them exactly what they're going to get and the exact benefits from those things. That's one of the problems people have with selling their core offers. A lot of times when we first go into a company that we buy or partner with they're just muddy in the deliverables. They're not explaining to the customer what it is they get and why they should care.

Sometimes the owner is so involved in doing everything in the business that they can't step away and look at their products, people, marketing or systems from a different perspective. Just our team coming into your office can be so helpful and give you an outside perspective because we love to answer your burning questions. When you're too close to your business, your product, you answer questions the customer didn't ask. It's about knowing what conversation is going on in your customer's head before they even realize it and connecting with them. It's about figuring out what they are really thinking. What questions are they really asking? Entering that conversation right then and there with this offer allows you to own the conversation. It's a no-brainer.

And the great big advantage that you have is that they just bought something. And because they bought something with the Tripwire you have a physiological reason why your core sale is so much easier. They just bought something from you. They're in a heaven/happy like place. It's actually a dopamine release. There is truly a shopper's high. When people buy something, it's akin to kissing. You actually have a dopamine release when you spend money. Consumerism is a disease, so to speak. And as soon as people spend money, whether it's $1, $10,

$5, they get a dopamine release. The more you spend, typically, the bigger the dopamine release.

So with the tripwire they get a little rush. They feel pretty good. Now offer something to them right away. After they have purchased the Tripwire, offer them your core product. If you don't take advantage of the emotional high at that moment, going back a week later and trying to get the sale is almost impossible. A week later, the emotional high is gone. So capture the moment.

Bringing It All Home

This leads me into the fourth part. It is critical for you to take full advantage of the buyer being in the right place, at the right time, in the right mindset so that they want to buy from you. You just show the benefit, you show the value and you want to tell them and describe to them exactly what they're going to get and for how much. You show the value in it and you compare it to other things so they can say for the price of a Starbucks coffee a day, you can own this new car or you can own this widget.

The fifth thing is what's called a "call to action" or CTA. I think this is really misunderstood. Most people, when they get down to the end of every one of these offers, are just asked to buy the product. What I am talking about here is a mindset and framing issue. A call to action to me is not asking someone to buy; it's *telling* someone to buy. "Now is the time to buy. I've explained the benefits to you and I truly believe, as a friend, that I'm doing you a favor by offering you my service." If you don't truly believe in your product, then you should probably sell something else. If I get that I'm giving you a service, then I'm going to be very firm in the end. I'm going to say, "Jimmy, I explained all this to you. Buddy, I know you need it. Let's go do this right now. Come on."

The EXIT Formula

I have found that most people, buyers especially, want to be told what to do. So tell them what you want them to do. Tell them to buy. This is what everybody wants. Everybody is afraid of telling the customer to buy; that's what he wants. He doesn't want you to ask him to make a decision. There's nothing people hate doing more than making a decision. The truth is, as much as I hate to say it, people just like to be told what to do. They do. They don't want to think. People are tired of thinking. We have to think all the time. We have to study all the time. We have to learn all the time. Just somebody tell me what to do….that builds trust.

Do you remember earlier when I talked about the customer value optimization process? It's where the person who is able and willing to spend the most money to acquire a customer wins. When you are able to spend more than everyone else, then you get all the traffic. If I am able and willing to spend the most to acquire a customer, then I can hire the best search engine optimization firm to go out and get me the best rankings. I can hire the best media buyers. I can hire the best pay per click people. Think about it like that. This is the game. You get this part right, every other aspect of business frankly becomes simple.

Imagine for a moment that I buy or partner with a company that is in your particular niche. Do you want to compete against us when we have all of this down to a science? Not if you are smart you don't. Sooner or later we will enter the same market you are in and no offense, but if you don't have these things implemented in your business then you're dead. You've got no shot. Why? Because I don't have to make any money on the front end because I have back-end products that are almost all profit. I can break even. That means I can buy all the PPC ads and all the Facebook ads I want. Plus, if I have money left over I'm going to put it in other areas of my marketing to sweeten my offers, to make my customers love me even more on the front of our relationship. I don't really want to make any money. I'd rather give it all back to them.

The End Results

The next step is what we call the "return path." So imagine that you started using a great lead magnet. And instead of getting two leads a day from your site/blog, now you're getting 50 leads a day from your site/blog. And how many of those customers buy your tripwire sale?

Because you made them a great tripwire sale, you have a 30%, 40%, 50% conversion rate to your core sale where you use to have a 4% or 5% conversion rate to your core sale. So you more than quadrupled, tripled, 10X, every step of this process moving forward. Every time you do that, it multiplies. It grows one upon itself. What could your company's profits look like?

You're getting more leads, you're making more sales, you're making more core sales, you've got more profit on the sales than you've ever made before. Now the last part is just getting the customer to come back and buy more often, right? That's it. The return path. The number one biggest asset in your business is your customer base, and it's the last place people look to build their businesses. It's the craziest thing.

The way that we work with most of the larger partners is by seeing how we can maximize Return on Investment (ROI) for them. So when we look at their business, we can look at their current existing customer base and usually figure out how to extract $10,000, $20,000, $50,000 $100,000, $200,000, $300,000 out of their existing list almost immediately.

So when they partner with us and give us equity, they don't feel like they are giving up much because of the growth that we are creating

The EXIT Formula

for the company and positioning the company for sale at a very large multiple. Essentially they are getting a smaller piece of a much larger pie:

- Customer Value Optimization (CV) – Lead magnets
- Tripwires
- Core Sale (irresistible offer)
- Offer Structure (benefits, value, product, cost)
- Call To Action (CTA)

When you are ready to get help with these items (regardless of the industry you are in), just contact us using the information at the end of this book. I would suggest if nothing else go ahead and fill out the application. You could get a lot of value from our review of your business.

This will definitely let you know where you are in your business. Just approaching your business in that way, I think, you're really going to get a lot out of it. But I invite you to turn it in. I would love to meet you and chat with you about your business, see what all you have going on even if it's not a great fit now, there may be a time in the near future where we can work together. And I'd like to do that. We love this stuff, and it's what we're really good at.

So I hope you got a lot out of this, especially if nothing else, I hope you did your own five things audit to see where you are and that you got something out of that part. And more than anything, I hope that we wind up working together.

Chapter 14

Customer Retention

So let's talk about customer return path. There are a few ways that you can get the customers to come back to you more often. Having constant contact with the customer is step one. Constant contact is super important. Don't be the company that only contacts your customer when you want to make a sale. You don't like companies or people who do that and neither does your customer. Just staying in constant contact with your customer is super important. Today it's so easy with email and with SMS text messaging, and then direct mail and a phone call every now and then. Just touching base and don't call to borrow money. Don't call necessarily to make a sale.

Here are some the ways of staying in contact with your customers that does not require a ton of effort:

A newsletter is an incredibly powerful tool to stay in contact with customers on a regular basis. But tell us a little bit about the business and a whole lot about what's going on in your life, what's going on with the growth of your company and other things that are of human interest. People are way more interested in those stories than they are with the sale you got going on.

They'll buy the thing from you if they know you, they like you and they trust you. It's really very simple. Remember those three words. Know, like, trust. Build that, and you have a new customer. And the biggest way that you can build that trust and that liking is by constant contact.

I want to go back to my good friend Howard Schultz, CEO of Starbucks. Starbucks, like a lot of super successful companies, employs loyalty programs to get customers to come back over and over again. They're doing pretty well. They sell the most commoditized thing in the world. Think about it. There's nothing more common on the face of the earth than coffee. But they built a multi-billion dollar business out of nothing, just by having loyalty programs. They applied this system to the biggest traditional common commodity around.

So loyalty programs give people discounts when they come back. Give them special treatment. Give them a holiday card, give them birthday gift cards, give them things that let them know that you appreciate them and because they're especially loyal customers, you're going to give them a special kind of treatment. That's the second way.

Another one is line extensions. Line extensions are just selling related products that maybe you don't make or commonly sell. At one point we bought a vitamin company. We wanted to grow it quickly and increase the size of the average customer order and get repeat buyers. So the first thing I said when I went in was "what else do you sell to your customers? What do your customers want?"

It turns out they were not selling any other products. They were not selling different sizes of their core product. They only had one travel size that barely fit in your refrigerator. They were not selling any other products that people who are health conscious want and need.

The challenge I see with so many companies we buy is that they sell only a single product, and they think their product defines who and what they are. The customer is what defines what your company is. Your customer defines your company, not by what you sell. And if you take that, your brain is going to explode because now you will have an endless supply of opportunities.

Here's what we did to solve that problem. We analyzed the customers buying patterns. We found out that customers who bought vitamins also bought many other items from other suppliers; things like clothes, additional vitamins, training programs, books and more. We figured out the top suppliers that sold those programs and called those companies and made a deal to be their rep. And while we only made a 15% or 20% margin, it was free money. We never had to touch the product.

The customer never went anywhere else. It became one-stop shopping for the customer. And the customer is coming back more regularly, so when they call us to buy vitamins now, guess what they buy? Some gels, clothes, other vitamins, books and training aids. But the cooler thing is, and this is what'll happen as you advance, a number of those items that we've sold as a dealer, now we're importing them or manufacturing them ourselves and we've just extended our line.

So that company just went from a growth of $1 million a year to approaching $3 million, with $4 million probably by the end of this year. All this been mainly accomplished by line extensions.

This next one is the key to evening out your monthly cash flow: Providing you with the capital you need each month to cover your basic overhead. If you do this part right, your business will change forever.

So here it is. I am talking about continuity programs. There is no better way to increase your transaction frequency that with the continuity program. It's impossible. There's no better way to do it. Because with the continuity program, a person is automatically buying whatever it is you're selling once a month or once a week or however often your continuity program dings them.

And traditional continuity programs are gym memberships, magazine subscriptions, tanning salons, Netflix, audio book clubs, cell phone companies, newsletters, book of the month club; things like that. They charge so much a month for their services. These businesses become behemoth companies. Utility companies, for lack of a better term, are really great big continuity programs. So they get monthly billing. And you'll notice that all the things I just said, what kind of companies are they? Extremely stable companies because they know they got their billings coming in the first of the month -no matter what happens.

Now you might be thinking "well, they don't really apply to my business." It absolutely does. I'm helping a student of mine buy large car washes. There are a lot of things the car wash is not doing to generate income and increase profits. So one of the things my student is going to do is implement a continuity program for the car wash. A continuity program is nothing more than having your customer pay you some amount of money each month whether they use your service or not. So in the car wash deal they are going to implement a monthly program where the customer can get unlimited car washes each month for $59. Everyone likes the idea because what does an average car wash cost? Around $25. So after just two washes you broke even. They have a couple of thousand continuity clients who pay that $60 each month, but only use it once a month. They know exactly what their monthly cash flow will be without ever having to find a new customer. New customers are icing on the cake. Which car wash do you think will be more valuable? One that depends on customers to drive by each day or one with 1,000 customers paying them $60 a month in advance? No comparison. The value of the business you build, that's a whole different conversation.

And I'll tell you, one of our goals, whether it's a company that we partner with or one that we purchase, is to have a two-day strategy session to figure out the best way to grow the company.

The EXIT Formula

Lack of a continuity program is one of the biggest reasons businesses struggle with their cash flow. 80% of the average business that starts in America today will be out of business in five years. Of those who survive, 80% of them will be out of business in another five years. Putting it in real numbers, if 500 businesses start today in America, in 10 years only 20 of them will still exist. The only exception to this is franchises. For instance, if 500 franchises start today, 460 of them will exist in 10 years.

So what's the difference? They have a plan. They have a strategy. They don't leave things to happenstance. So whether you partner or sell to us or do it yourself, you need to get a plan together. You don't have to believe in yourself. You don't have to believe in us. You don't have to believe in any of the things I'm talking about. This is mathematics, and the numbers don't lie.

The EXIT Formula

Chapter 15

Networking Your Way to Millions

Have you ever heard of the book *Rich Dad, Poor Dad* by Robert Kiyosaki? He thinks differently than everybody else, and of course he gets different results than everybody else. I originally read Robert's book over 20 years ago. It was a book that dramatically changed my life. He admits that instead of working in the business, work on the business and grow a business rather than doing all of the little stuff. You have to think differently. Not only did I read that book but I also read *Rich Dad for Kids, Building Businesses,* and *Real Estate.* I've read just about all of them. Another great book that I liked a lot was *The Art of the Deal* by Donald Trump, which was awesome.

 Let's get started with the education here. So what does it take to succeed in today's market? It takes one person, one deal and one opportunity to change your life and take your business to the next level. When you look back at this, your friendships will lead to so many great relationships. That's all it takes. You look back and remember it's that one person, that one coach or that one partner that made a difference, that one deal that put you on your path that changed forever. Or this bigger deal that helped you take it to the next level with this big business and then the opportunity, an event that I went to or extra follow-up and follow through. That's what life is all about.

Does the number 212 mean anything to you? It turns out that at 212 degrees, water is very hot. At 212 degrees, it produces steam. Steam can drive a train. What would happen if you start raising your potential one degree at a time? Here we're not talking about changing everything. We're talking about adding one degree; one degree and the importance of adding that steam. That one degree that will just change everything forever. It's changing one degree at a time to make that happen. The more you power, the more steam there is, the more power you have. That's what we're going to do. We're going to change people's business one degree at a time.

There are many ways to grow any business, but here are three ways that I grow my business in real estate, e-commerce, manufacturing, SAS, professional services and more:

1) Increase the number of clients.
2) Increase the average transaction value. The bigger deals they do with you, the more money you can make. The more products and services they buy from you the more money you make.
3) Increase the frequency of repurchasing or investing with you. You get more residual value from each client. We talked about this. 90% of your business will come from 10% of your relationships. It costs seven times more to get a new partner or new customer than it does to work on an existing one.

You want to grow your business one degree at a time, so use those three things and you're going to see you have a steam full of business.

Think about this for a moment. Guaranteeing purchases through risk reversal. I coach people and am known as one of the top coaches in the United States (and maybe the world right now) in business acquisition and growth, and definitely one of the highest paid ones, so this is very easy for me. Why? I added a risk reversal. What if you guaranteed people by saying something like "Hey, listen, if the deal loses money, I'll cover it." So minimize the risk, especially in a new relationship. Host beneficial relationships or have other people introduce you to their lists or infiltrate circles of influence through marketing. Say "here is my good friend Mike Warren. Here's the guy that we really trust." You're dealing with host beneficial relationships here.

Be A Good Storyteller

It is important to understand that facts tell and stories sell. That's one of the important things. You could have a great proposal, but stories are what sell. People want to know about you, and some of the best stories are five to six sentences long. Those rambling people... really it's not very effective. Stories help you sell yourself and your product without really selling it. Stories which people can relate to or see themselves are most effective and profitable. That's one thing that I've really seen effective for branding. I want what you want, or I can see myself buying that or being that. For example, "Are you having back problems? Are you having trouble sleeping at night? Are you restless all night? Hi, Billy Mays here for the 'Fill in the blank.'" Or people say "Would you like to live this lifestyle? Would you like to be this?" People want to relate to that. "How would you like to be stress-free?" This is very effective. You can learn a lot from watching infomercials, because it makes a huge, huge, huge difference in how you do things.

I have stories for all different scenarios. Let me share seven of them with you right now. There are more, but these seven will get you started. You need to have stories in the back of your mind that you can pull out depending on who you are talking to. In other words, have different stories for different facts. Have a minimum of seven introduction stories in the back of your mind. When people ask "What's your story?" you'll have the story of who you are, why you are who you are, and what you've done. You've got to have it, not just wing it. It has to be interesting. It has to be tight and concise. What is

The EXIT Formula

the key to success? Practice plus preparation plus visualization equals success.

When people ask "What's your story?" I've got a type story. I practice it. I've prepared it and I can make it engaging because if people ask me, they're interested. So here are my 7 Stories:

1. **Attention Story.** That's a dramatic story that has a "wow" appeal to it that is so unbelievable. These stories are meant to show people why they should listen to you. For example, when you hear my story or I'm teaching something, people say "Wow, that's impressive. I want to learn from that." When people say "wow" they want to learn more. They want to be around you. They want to inquire more which could lead to a sell, an investment or an introduction, so having a "wow" story is very important.

2. **Money Story.** You want to show how people, by doing business with you or your product, are going to make money safely and securely. That's what people want to know, "How am I going to make money?" Do you have a story of how you have helped a client or partnered with someone to make money? That is very important in the marketplace today and a huge credibility factor.

3. **Fear Stories.** Fear stories or other horror stories your clients have experienced, but when they came on board with you it all changed. For example, "I bought a product from this person, and I got burned. The course didn't teach me anything. Then I went with Mike (or your company) and here is the result. They made me believe again." A common story is "I invested with somebody else, and I got burned." You've got to say "You know, it's interesting. I have a partner whose name is John. He went through the exact same thing and now here is what he is

doing." This is called "branding by association."

4. **Ego Stories.** Ego stories show your partner or customer that if they use your product it can help them increase their self-confidence or help them manage their risk better because they will be able to trust better. Some people ask, "How do I make more money?" They want a bigger car, a bigger house, more respect. You want to play up to that and play to their ego. It's a very effective story depending on what type of people you are talking with at that moment. Different people, different things; it's important to know who you're dealing with.

5. **Increased Productivity Stories.** How many times have you met someone and said "I'd love to get to it but I just don't have the time to get involved?" This is where you've got to tell them it's an "earn more and work less" story. You've got to give them a story about how they can get involved, but they're not going to do any of the work. You have to make that association. You can't just say "You won't do the work, I will." You have to tell them through stories. Stories are so powerful in convincing people to invest with you and do business with you.

6. **We Are Together Stories.** We are moving away from an idealist society to a community's society, with people adding value essential to their business. There are people who tell me they can make me a lot of money, but they haven't made any money themselves. That's the first sign of someone that is an amateur in the marketplace today. But sometimes people don't care about making money. Maybe the story you're telling them is about how they're going to make the environment better or increase the quality of neighborhoods or show how they can provide affordable housing. Maybe part of the money is going to go to a charity. It's always important to find out the 'why' of the individual.

7. **Security Stories.** In this time of Ponzi schemes, WorldCom, and Madoff, many people are skeptical. How are you different than these people? How are your potential partners protected? As I see it, that's a big concern in today's market. Credibility is huge, especially now, because of so much negative publicity. You have to do it differently.

Networking In A Warm Market

You can use your connections to find partners for deals. You can gain access to unlimited funds for projects or investing your company. You can get access to relational capital that I will be talking about later. You can gain access to resources you don't have access to and can't develop on your own.

To be successful in networking you've got to get other people to sell you. Write this down: it is always, always better when someone sells you than when you sell yourself. How do you find partners? Warm markets.

Warm markets are your friends, your family, and your business connections. Warm markets don't like to be pitched. You should never, ever ask them for money. Instead, ask them for an introduction. "Can you please introduce me to someone who can help me in my business?" This works 60% of the time, which means eliminate the word "referral" from your vocabulary. It is always better to ask someone for an introduction rather than a referral, which implies work.

Now, before you ask your warm market for an introduction, you must appear to be the expert in your field or know what you're talking about. If not, your market will be reluctant to introduce you to anybody. Nobody wants to make the introduction if they don't have that confidence that you know what you're talking about. Is that right? Because then they're going to look bad and that person is going to say "Why did you send me this idiot?" I've seen it so many times before. The point is to come across like you know what you're talking about in your market.

Think about this: the more you give, the more you get. Content driven individuals and substance tend to do very well. People don't just want snippets. Give them the great content, give them the value, and make that proposition on the value rather than the other way around. You want to make connections for them based on their whys and their needs. That makes a very, very big difference. You also want to be the connector and monetize the connection.

A good networker usually gets paid back ten times more than he or she has put in. You also want to make your partners or people you do business with look good. The more you make other people look good, the more they are going to want to make you look good. It's called "a reciprocal relationship." And remember, you have to instigate the big picture vision. Paint them a picture. Wealthy people like others who know how to do the heavy lifting.

Here is a method that might help you to remember how to network. I call it the *IRS* model:

I = Informative
R = Relevant
S = Stand Out

When you first meet someone, be Informative about yourself as well as your business. Try to be Relevant to each person you speak to. In others words, provide value to them. Stand Out from others vying for your prospects. Once you've perfected the *IRS* model you will become memorable, you will become the expert, and you will become the go-to person. You will have the upper hand on your competition.

Being Pitch Perfect

I don't like to rely on scripts. However, in the beginning it is important for you to know your pitch or your "ice breaker." Let me give you a few examples of how to network with multi-millionaires:

- Step One: "Hi, my name is Mike Warren." Then add a compliment, congratulation or a statement. "Hi, John, my name is Mike Warren and congratulations. Tom Smith told me you and your son caught a 6-point buck." Or "Congratulations John on your new book. I really liked the chapter on mindsets. It reminded me of when I took my business to the next level." Every event you're at is different, so you have to be eight steps ahead of everyone else.
- Step Two: The conversation starter must be thought out and relevant, topical and one that does not require a 'yes' or 'no' reply. Ask them questions like, "John, what are the hot topics in today's' economy?" "John, what do you think about the new job bill being released? Will it affect your business?" You want to elicit a response from them, one that will keep the conversation going
- Step Three: Ask them about what is most important to them. Ask them about their success story. Ask them about how they built their business. People love talking about themselves.
- Step Four: If the person asks, "So Mike, what do you do?" and it took at least ten minutes before that question got asked, you're in great shape. You are more likely to be successful and impactful. If someone asks you after five minutes, that means they're just trying to move the conversation and they're not interested. Less than two minutes would just be a formality.

Whenever they asked me what I do after ten minutes of general conversation, I know I've got them.
- Step Five: This is where you insert your 30 second presentation, your "elevator pitch." The biggest problem about entrepreneurs and real estate investors is that they just wing it and that becomes a big problem, so having a 30 second elevator pitch is critical to keeping the conversation moving.
- Step Six: Be ready for objections. You tell them you're in real estate and they say, "Oh, it's a horrible time" or "You can't make money. Banks are not lending right now."
- Step Seven: You have to cover the objection. Objection based marketing. The same objections come up every time, so are you ready for them? If you're ready for the objections, then you're more likely to be impactful.
- Step Eight: It's your time to shine. You want to showcase your knowledge of what you do, yourself and your business. Use statements or stories to illustrate your points. Remember: facts tell, stories sell. So if someone says "I'm interested in real estate. What kind of money are we talking about?" Then you give him a money story. If someone is interested, give them an Introduction story. This may lead to a Wow story or a Fear story or an Ego story. Be eight steps ahead of everyone else.
- Step Nine: Be the one who ends the conversation. "Thank you very much, Mr. Jones. That was a fascinating conversation. I'd love to chat with you again and help you with your new business venture." Adding value to what their 'why' is will make a huge difference in the marketplace.
- Step Ten: If you made a good impression you will be watched. They watch how you interact with others. If you crushed it with this script, don't go to another person and do the exact same thing with the exact same story. That person might go back and

compare notes with the others. You don't want someone saying: "Oh, that guy had a canned speech." People are always looking for faults.

Network Your Way to millions.

What do you know? Who do you know? Who knows you? How can you add value to them or their business or their life? What do others value about you? How are you different than your competitors? What are your "wows?" What is your USP? That's how you network your way to millions. That is how you get people to give you money for deals, business, and joint ventures.

Tell me who your friends are, and I'm going to tell you who you are. Your network equals your net worth. Write that down. **Your network equals your net worth.** Take the average of your five closest friends or people who you hang around with and write down their net worth, and that's what you're worth now or you're going to be worth. Who you hang out with is who you become because your belief leads to your behaviors and your behaviors lead to your results. Fire the negative people around you. Start hanging with people that you can build up to and the more you hang out with people that are more successful, the more successful you become because you start adapting.

Chapter 16

How to Get All the Guidance You Need

You have read a lot in this book and by now I am sure you are pretty darn excited about going out there to grow your company or even to grow your company through acquisition. If you are interested in having our firm help do all of this for you so that you can focus on running your company, then please visit our website and fill out a simple questionnaire. We will contact you and get the discussion going. We only partner with companies that are willing to give up some equity to make the deal work. Please note that the amount may be negotiable.

I do want to take a moment and talk about equity. A lot of people get hung up on giving up equity in their company. They have heard lots of horror stories or have heard from their cousin Joe that they should never do that. So let me tackle this objection this way:

Equity really only comes into play if the company is sold. If we can grow your company so that you receive a smaller piece of a larger pie later, is it worth it to you to have someone else do all the work?

Great companies don't work for free, and neither do we. If you want an SEO company, you can go online and find one. You can spend thousands of dollars and months of wasted time and get no results. You end up bouncing from one provider to another with no results. Additionally, you still are missing many other pieces that you need to triple your profit.

If you want a commission based sales person, then that is not us. If you are looking for an affiliate for your products, that is also not us. We grow companies and take them to the next level, allowing the owner (you) to sell your company for far more than you thought possible.

We have the teams in these different areas that have proven track records. You can try and do all of this on your own, but honestly if you could do it all, why are you reading this book? I am not trying to be harsh. I am just trying to get real and be direct with you.

The above is almost like a "don't work with us" slogan. The reality is, we can only work with a few companies at a time. We want companies with owners who see the value in what we have to offer and are willing to participate with us to reach our joint goals. Each company is unique, and so are you. If this is you then great, please fill out our application and get started. I don't want to waste your time with false promises that we can help everybody.

The next step you might want to consider is a strategy session. This is where we go into the companies we partner with or purchase and work with the key employees. We typically do a two-day session where we bring in our team of experts and break down the company on the first day to find out what is working for the company and what's not working. On day two, we rebuild the company by throwing out what is not working and improving on what is working and implementing new strategies that will literally double the business in about six months.

One of the goals that we set as an initial strategy is to ask ourselves "how can we get the continuity billings to cover all the overhead cost completely?"

Imagine how great this would feel. When you walk into the month knowing you're good, all the bills are paid, that very first sale you make is going to go into your pocket. I don't care how big your company is.

I don't care if you have a small six-figure business or a multi-billion dollar business. When you walk into the month knowing all your bills are paid by a continuity program, by past customers, it completely changes the economics of your business. I keep saying that phrase; changing the economics of business because it all goes back to that singular goal of "how can we engineer this process?"

That's what Hyper-Growth is all about. How can we engineer your business without necessarily adding a bunch of these things? We're not acquiring any business; we're not getting bank loans. Without doing all the stuff that you don't necessarily have any control over, how can we engineer the business based on what we'll have today so that you are able to spend the most money in your entire niche to acquire a customer? And if you started to do that, you would win. So ultimately this is what we do. If you would like us to do this for your company and achieve hyper-growth, prepare your company to be sold and finally sell it for much more than it is worth today, then contact us using the information at the back of this book.

I'll tell you a little bit about how the process works when we do wind up working together. Coming back to the five things I mentioned earlier, we look at those five things. And we analyze your business, and we see which ones you have, which ones you don't have. We'll do an initial implementation and analysis of the five things.

And we figure out which one of the five is going to have the greatest potential. If we optimize one part over another, what's going to happen? How is it going to happen? Now, I tell you, what we just covered for the compounding effect, typically, we're going to start with the lead or at helping develop tripwires. But that's how it's going to work. We work together to take one of these five things at a time and we just plow through the business until every single one of your

The EXIT Formula

five things is fully optimized. And it really is a puzzle. It's a lot of fun. We have a lot of fun doing it, and I know you're going to have a lot of fun, not only with the process but with the success that's achieved afterward.

Conclusion

I want to thank you so much for taking the time to read my book. I hope it has enlightened you, surprised you and maybe even more importantly motivated and inspired you. If you are truly serious about finally tasting the fruits of independence, taking your company to the next level at last and finally being the master of your own destiny, then using the techniques covered in this book will help you achieve your goals. Take the next step toward freedom and a true measure of happiness.

Good luck, happy hunting and let us know of your success!

# The EXIT Formula

Bonus Chapter

Questions Buyers Ask

In this chapter you will find a collection of the most common questions that buyers have asked in the transactions that I've been involved in, such as:

- What are net sales?
- Have you been in business for 3+ years?
- Is there a big market for your product?
- Do you have financial statements? (Buyers prefer audited but will settle for compiled)
- Do you sell something customers need and already know they need?
- Is there a high upside?
- Is the business currently running at a low percentage of capacity?
- Is it a low-tech business? (not changing rapidly, low risk of obsolescence)
- Is it a low skills business that does not require highly skilled people that are highly paid and difficult to find?
- Is it currently profitable or running at a net loss?
- Can sourcing raw materials or product improve profit margins?
- Does it currently have bad marketing that is easy to improve?
- Are financial accounting and reporting systems in place now?
- Are you or can you locate an experienced manager if the owner/CEO leaves the company?
- Will owner stay on for 2-3 years?
- How can the owner be replaced with permanent staff that will transfer to new owners when you sell?
- Is the owner open to trading equity for our value-added skills

and resources?
- Is the owner okay with an asset transfer to a new company or the creation of a new company for new channels?
- Does the company own all of its IP? (Intellectual Property)
- Who are the key employees?
- Will they stick around after acquisition?
- If not, who can perform their functions/duties?
- How hard is it to replace them internally or externally?
- Is there any litigation threatened or pending?
- Are the payroll, sales and income taxes current?
- Are there any environmental issues with you company?
- Are there any family members involved in the business? If there are any, determine their role. Are they employees or shareholders? Are they expecting or hoping to stay on? If there are family members, why isn't the business being sold to them? Learn if these family members have a say in the negotiation.
- To what level can the business be built? This is a trick question (fasten your seatbelt for this one). Sellers will typically say: "The sky's the limit. With the right person, this business can be doubled or tripled... easily." It has to make you wonder – if this is so, why didn't they do it? Or, are they simply the wrong person? While their answer will almost certainly be embellished, this is a good time to corner them and ask: "If that's possible, please tell me specifically what would have to happen to achieve that kind of growth?"
- Why haven't they expanded the business? There may be some indication that could relate to areas of potential growth, i.e. skill, knowledge, ability, or lack of any of these, etc.
- What is the profile of the ideal candidate to take over and build this business? (Strengths, background, etc.) (This is a good example of why you will pose your questions first. If you don't,

they may very well gear their answers to fit you, which is something you do not want them to do. You'll decide this on your own without their influence. Try and pick up certain specifics that they may allude to, as opposed to generalities. For example, hard-working, honest and reliable is evasive. However, sales-oriented, with a good background in product development, is specific. Undoubtedly, they will say that if the business has someone aggressive behind it, there are all kinds of things that can be done. Then again, this can be said of every business. Push them for particular skills.)

- Do they like the business and what do they like most and least? (This should give you some insight into the tasks that the current owner has been focusing on. Typically, they will like what they are best at and dislike what they are not. Human nature being what it is; they will be spending the most time on what they enjoy. If this is not the "driver" of the business, you will have an indication that the business has some room for improvements, based on the fact that the majority of their time may not have been devoted to what is most critical.)

Once you have gone through the questions, you should have a pretty darn good idea of the questions that a buyer may ask you.

Seller Questionnaire (for online businesses)

In the main program, we will be discussing all of the key questions to ask the seller of any business. We also outline the rationale behind the questions, and the answers to look out for during your meetings or conversations with them. Nevertheless, there are a number of critical questions specific to the operation of an online business that we'll discuss here.

The EXIT Formula

Make sure that whenever you are talking to the seller that you have your questions well prepared and take flawless notes. I guarantee that you will need to review them during the buying process.

The questions you ask the seller and the answers they provide (subject to your further validation, of course) will form an enormous part of your evaluation of the business. Quite often an online business is really a "one man show" and so it will be especially important for you to learn if you can easily assume all of the tasks they perform.

Also, it is common to find sellers who started the business, built the website from scratch, often by trial and error and "bolted on" functions to the website and operating backend system. As such, you'll want to know who operates the technical side of it now, how easy is it to learn, can a stranger effectively take it over, and how simple are the guts of the business? Or, as my good friend Bill Miller always asks: "Is it a big plate of spaghetti?"

Once you get a handle on the technical side of things, you'll want to drill down to learn what you're "really" buying. Unless the business has proprietary products or technology, it may very well be that the entire business is simply a marketing play. That can be fine, but again, you need to know what separates this business from the competition, and is it sustainable? Also, how easily can someone else enter this space and become your competitor?

You will also need to know:
- What is your technical background?
- What drives the sales in this business?
- What parts of the business do you outsource?
- What functions within the business are automated, and which are handled manually?

- Who did the original setup and/or programming of the website? (If not the owner, you will need to speak to that person at the appropriate time).
- What are the typical challenges presented to completing a sale? Please outline the sales process.
- How do people find out about your website?
- Who are the main competitors?
- How many unique visitors do you get every month? How are these tracked? Can I see the reports?
- What is your conversion rate? What is the industry conversion rate?
- How have conversion rates trended in the past three years?
- To what do you attribute the trends either way?
- What is the website's primary objective? Is it Sales? Leads? Subscriptions? Opening sale and then backend sale?
- How many clients do you have in your database?
- Once you sell a customer something, is there an ongoing dialog with them? What about any Backend sales?
- What other products can you add to the mix?
- What are your main marketing/advertising campaigns? PPC, affiliates?
- Who manages the advertising and marketing? How do they do it?
- How do you know if campaigns are successful?
- How does the company rank in the search engines' organic listings and who handles the website's optimization?
- How competitive is the field?
- Do you have any proprietary products? Systems? Software?
- What client records do you maintain? If credit card information is stored, how are they secured?

The EXIT Formula

- Who handles your credit card processing? How much is your monthly credit card line? Very important because you will need to get these lines of credit in place - they will NOT just transfer over to you.
- How are orders and payments processed?
- How easily can a competitor enter this field?
- Do you own your server?
- When your website goes down, how are you notified?
- What is your disaster plan?
- How is the company data backed up? How often? Who does it? How?
- What is the backend software? Who operates/maintains it? If the owner, how will it transition? If an employee, will he or she stay?
- Are you involved in any other Internet businesses?
- Since the Internet operates globally, are you willing to sign a worldwide non-compete?
- When fully automated, an online business can be the ideal absentee run business. Why are you selling?
- What do you see as the future trends in this industry?
- Are there any brick and mortar companies in this business?
- Do you see any possibility that a brick and mortar presence will ultimately be needed for the business?
- Do any of your suppliers (if applicable) sell directly through their own website to your customer base?
- Can this business be relocated easily?
- When you travel, how does the business operate?
- Please explain how you arrived at the asking price and terms?
- Are you the "face" of the business? Do people identify you with or as the business?

About the Author

Mike Warren is an international business maverick whose contrarian strategies have helped his students generate tremendous growth and increase cash flow for their businesses. His students and clients come from a variety of different backgrounds but primarily are C-level executives and entrepreneurs. He specializes in getting cash for businesses and real estate, as well as buying and selling companies across the world. Students from around the world are passionate to learn Mike's proven strategies.

Mike speaks, trains, and coaches both nationwide and internationally about real estate, hyper-business growth, and credit. His presentation style has been described as edutainment: a mix of education and entertainment. He teaches through platform, teleseminar, webinar and video conferencing. He is the bestselling author of "How To Buy A Business Using Its Own Cash," an in-depth how-to book to get into the "business flipping" game.

The EXIT Formula

To learn more about how you can work with Mike, visit him at his website at **http://www.TimeEquityGroup.com**.

You can also find other books authored by Mike Warren at **http://amazon.com**

Printed in Great Britain
by Amazon